the secret of staying in love

the secret
of
staying in love

JOHN POWELL, S.J.

ARGUS COMMUNICATIONS

Allen, Texas 75002

This book is gratefully dedicated to

Bernice Brady.

Bee has been a great source of support
in many of my previous attempts to write.
She has generously contributed an excellent
critical eye, a cultivated literary sense,
and especially a confident kind of encouragement.
She was unequalled as a proofreader.

She did not help with the preparation of this book.
On June 11, 1973,
Bee received a "better offer."
She was called by the Author and Lord
of the Universe to join the celebration
at the banquet of eternal life.

Even in your absence, you were present, Bee.
This one is for you.

Acknowledgments

Excerpt from *Man's Search for Meaning* by Viktor Frankl. Beacon Press, Boston.

Excerpt from *Modern Man in Search of a Soul* by C. G. Jung. Harcourt Brace Jovanovich, New York.

Excerpts from *The Art of Loving* by Erich Fromm, Vol. 9 in *World Perspectives.* Edited by Ruth Nanda Anshen. Copyright © 1956 by Erich Fromm. By permission of Harper Row. These excerpts also reprinted with the permission of George Allen & Unwin, Ltd., London.

Excerpt from *Escape From Freedom* by Erich Fromm. Holt, Rinehart & Winston, New York.

Excerpt from *Markings* by Dag Hammarskjöld translated by Lief Sjoberg and W. H. Auden. Copyright © 1964 by Alfred A. Knopf, Inc. and Faber & Faber, Ltd. Reprinted by permission of Alfred A. Knopf, Inc. This excerpt also reprinted with the permission of Faber & Faber, Ltd., London.

Excerpt from *Conceptions of Modern Psychiatry* by Dr. Harry Stack Sullivan. W. W. Norton & Co., Inc., New York.

Excerpts reprinted from *Letters to a Young Poet* by Rainer Maria Rilke translation by M. D. Herter Norton. By permission of W. W. Norton & Company, Inc. Copyright 1934 and 1954 by W. W. Norton & Company, Inc. Copyright renewed 1962 by M. D. Herter Norton. These excerpts also reprinted with the permission of the Hogarth Press, Ltd., London.

Excerpt from *The Miracle of Dialogue* by Reuel Howe. Seabury Press, New York.

contents

CHAPTER ONE

Be patient toward all that is unsolved
    in your heart . . .
Try to love the questions themselves . . .

Do not now seek the answers,
            which cannot be given
            because you would not be able
            to live them.
And the point is,
            to live everything.

Live the questions now.
Perhaps you will then
            gradually,
            without noticing it,
Live along some distant day
            into the answers.

Rainer Maria Rilke

the human condition
needs
options
addictions

My Sisters and Brothers
in our Human Family:
   I am writing again because I think I have something to say to you. Perhaps you have read something which I have written previously. It is not important, really. What I wrote then reflected where I was
then as a person. This book is to share with you
where I have gone from that point, where I am now.
What I really want to say to you is that I think I have
lived along into some new insights and answers,

and I want to share them with you, to have your reaction to them. There are, of course, many questions about the mystery of me, the mystery of you and the mystery of our relationship which are still unsolved in my heart. There are so many questions which I must continue to love because I am as yet unable to live their answers.

In the periods of waiting for answers, we can feel very small and helpless. We can feel dominated and intimidated by the "professionals" who have the necessary degrees and "credentials" to instruct us. I would like to assure you that I do not come as one of these. I do not come as a teacher but as a brother. I hold out my offering, the offering of myself, in trembling, uncertain hands. Whatever is helpful, please keep as yours. Let whatever is not helpful sift and slip softly through your fingers.

human needs

I am convinced that man was meant to live at peace within himself, filled with a deep joy. I am convinced that there should be going on in the heart of every man not a funeral but a celebration of life and love. Prophets of gloom, with their "valley of tears" mentality and vocabulary, have always sounded unreal to me. With good old St. Irenaeus of the second century I have always believed that "The glory of God is a man fully alive!" Of course, there is no problemless Camelot or painless Utopia. The tension resulting from problems and pain is part of the whole piece, and usually directs our attention to a growing-edge of life, a territory for expansion. For myself, I do not regret the problems or pain in my past life, but only the apathy, the moments when I was not "fully alive."

The essential sadness of our human family is that very few of us even approach the realization of our full potential. I accept the estimate of the theoreticians that the average person accomplishes only 10% of his promise. He sees only 10% of the beauty in the world about him. He hears only 10% of the music and poetry in the universe. He smells only a tenth of the world's fragrance, and tastes only a tenth of the deliciousness of being alive. He is only 10% open to his emotions, to tenderness, to wonder and awe. His mind embraces only a small part of the thoughts, reflections and understanding of which he is capable. His heart is only 10% alive with love. He will die without ever having really lived or really loved. To me this is the most frightening of all possibilities. I would really hate to think that you or I might die without having really lived and really loved.

the sadness of failure

If we were made to be fully alive, why do we so often find ourselves reduced to making the best of a bad thing? Obviously, in our lives and in the lives of so many others something needed for the fullness of life is missing or at least is not being recognized and enjoyed. Somehow, somewhere, something has gone wrong. Somewhere along the way the light has failed. In his verse, "Out of Order," André Auw describes his reactions when he comes upon the scene of a young mother trying to explain to her four-year-old boy that the popcorn machine cannot give out its contents:

"You can't get any popcorn, Child. The
    machine is out of order. See, there
    is a sign on the machine."

But he didn't understand. After all, he had the
    desire, and he had the money, and he
    could see the popcorn in the machine.
    And yet somehow, somewhere, something
    was wrong because he couldn't get the
    popcorn.

The boy walked back with his mother, and he
    wanted to cry.

And Lord, I too felt like weeping, weeping for
    people who have become locked-in,
    jammed, broken machines filled with
    goodness that other people need and
    want and yet will never come to enjoy,
    because somehow, somewhere,
    something has gone wrong inside.

All forms of life have optimum conditions and essential requirements for health, growth, the fullness
of life. When the environment of each being fur-
nishes these conditions and requirements, the fullness of life is possible, the potential riches can be
realized. When people are fully alive, saying a vi-
brant *yes* to the full human experience and a full-
hearted *amen* to love, there is an indication that their
human needs are being met. But when the contrary
is true, when discomfort, frustration and crippling
emotions take over in a human life, there is a contra-
indication that the human needs of these people are
not being met. It may be through their own failure or
through the failure of those closest to them, but they
are just not getting what they need. Somehow,
somewhere, something has gone wrong in those
lives. Starvation and disintegration have set in.

the fundamental
human need

Man is not simple. He is a composite of body, mind and spirit, and he has needs on all three levels of his existence. He has needs and appetites that are physical, psychological and spiritual. Frustration at any one of these levels can produce agony in the whole organism.

However, there is a growing consensus of opinion that there is one need so fundamental and so essential that if it is met, everything else will almost certainly harmonize in a general sense of well-being. When this need is properly nourished, the whole human organism will be healthy and the person will be happy. This need is *a true and deep love of self, a genuine and joyful self-acceptance, an authentic self-esteem,* which result in *an interior sense of celebration:* "It's good to be me. . . . I am very happy to be me!"

Did something in you become immediately uncomfortable and uneasy when you read the previous statement? Conditioned as we are by our culture, we seem to be emotionally allergic to the very vocabulary of love of self. The thought of rejoicing in and celebrating our own unique goodness seems like a very distant and alien thought. Immediate associations of egotism, vanity and selfishness rush like dark clouds into our minds. I suspect that most of us never get through the crust of this difficult vocabulary and these suspicions to find the most important reality of any human life and the beginning of all human love.

Sometimes I wonder if it is the reality of self-love and self-appreciation that threatens us as much as the anticipated reaction of others. We might think that others would reject us if self-esteem ever floated to the surface of our communications. As an experiment with our societal attitude towards self-acceptance, I once introduced myself to my university class, on our first day together, as someone who really accepted, believed in and loved himself. I told them that I was a very good person, kind, generous, and loving. I assured them of my adequate intelligence, and of my instinctual feeling that I am a good teacher with a stimulating message. I tried to do this in a sincere, factual, and honest manner.

Some of my students laughed nervously, wondering if I could possibly be serious, while others fixed me with a stare that wondered: Should we shoot him or spray him? One girl, who appeared to be on the verge of nausea, turned to the person sitting next to her and announced not too silently: "Yuk! What conceit!" After this extended self-introduction as the kind of teacher you always wanted but were afraid to expect, I began to present the material of the course. Only in the following class period did I explain my experiment to the students. (Even to this day I have never been fully sure that all of them believed the explanation.) Anyway, I invited them to re-listen to their emotional reactions to my self-introduction. "Were you happy that I could openly acknowledge and publicly admit my self-appreciation? Were you able to join me in my celebration of being me? Or did you feel resentment, suspicion?" I tried to convince my students that their reactions were telling them something about themselves, about our society and about how we react to expressed love of self.

In his book, *Escape from Freedom,* Erich Fromm insists that the egotism, vanity, and conceit which we are constantly suspecting in one another are re-

ally the very opposite of true self-love, self-acceptance and self-celebration.

Selfishness is not identical with self-love but its very
opposite. Selfishness is one kind of greediness. Like all
greediness, it contains an insatiability, as a
consequence of which there is never any real
satisfaction. Greed is a bottomless pit which exhausts
the person in an endless effort to satisfy the need without
ever reaching satisfaction. . . . the selfish person is
always anxiously concerned with himself; he is never
satisfied, is always restless, always driven by the fear of
not getting enough, of missing something, of being
deprived of something. He is filled with burning envy of
anyone who might have more. . . . this type of person is
basically not fond of himself at all, but deeply dislikes
himself. . . . Selfishness is rooted in this very lack of
fondness for oneself. . . . narcissism, like selfishness, is
an overcompensation for the basic lack of
self-love. . . . He loves neither others nor himself.

We have here a question that each of us must
silently, reflectively consider. What are my true feelings? When I hear something complimentary about
another, why do I say: "Don't tell him. It might go to
his head"? Why do I not want others to be happy with
themselves? I don't want "it" to go to his head. What
is "it" that I don't want in the head of my brother or
sister? What *do* I want in his head? If another re-
joices in some success, why do I immediately accuse him of bragging? Why have I become such a
jealous guardian of his humility? Why does it concern me so much?

Perhaps the answer to these and similar questions will lead me to the realization that I do not want
him to love himself because I am unable to love
myself. It is a psychological truism that our attitudes
towards others are conditioned by our fundamental

attitudes towards ourselves. If I cannot openly and honestly acknowledge my own strengths and assets, I will not want anyone else to acknowledge his. You and I must sit for a while and ponder this question because the answer may be seriously crippling or slowly destroying us. Everything depends upon and flows from our openness to ourselves. When we lose the ability to appreciate ourselves and enjoy being ourselves, all sorts of dark and painful things rush in to fill the void.

As you ramble through life, my Brother,
Whatever be your goal,
Keep your eye upon the doughnut,
And not upon the hole.

Bertrand Russell once said, "A man cannot possibly be at peace with others until he has learned to be at peace with himself." Rabbi Joshua Liebman has advocated a rewording of the biblical command of love so that it will read: "Love and believe in yourself properly and you will love and believe in your neighbor." A psychiatrist-spokesman for the Payne-Whitney Psychiatric Clinic in New York has been quoted as saying: "If people had a healthy love of themselves instead of hating themselves and feeling bad, if only they would love the child in themselves instead of despising the weakness, our case load would be cut in half."

Most contemporary psychotherapy, as typified in the current enthusiasm for Transactional Analysis and its central goal of learning to feel Okay, is designed to help a person towards one thing: to help him adopt a kindly, positive and accepting attitude towards himself. Most people are very far from this, even though we could easily be deceived by surface attitudes. From a literal reading of these surface attitudes, we might wrongly conclude that most

"It's good to be me . . . .
I am very happy to be me!"

people really do love themselves. On the surface, most of us accuse and attack others while justifying ourselves. However, deep down in areas which we are normally afraid to confront and explore, the exact opposite is true. We give others a probation or extended sentence while we "throw the book at" ourselves. A psychiatrist at the Mental Health Clinic of the University of South Carolina medical school has said that "Our biggest job is to help patients find out what is good about themselves. It never fails: as they begin to like themselves a little better, they begin simultaneously to get well."

Dr. Robert H. Felix, the former director of the National Institute for Mental Health, describes this healthy love and acceptance of self as a ". . . feeling of dignity, of belonging, a feeling of worthwhileness, a feeling of adequacy." Dr. Felix continues: "We must learn to regard ourselves with understanding. I must learn to enjoy being myself. I would not want to be anyone else. I would want to be only myself."

There is no doubt in my mind that a deep understanding of and a serious effort to achieve true love of self is the beginning of all human growth and happiness. In our efforts to establish this as fact, we would finally like to quote the great psychiatrist Carl G. Jung, from his book *Modern Man in Search of a Soul:*

Perhaps this sounds very simple, but simple things are always the most difficult. In actual life it requires the greatest discipline to be simple, and the acceptance of self is the essence of the moral problem and the epitome of a whole outlook upon life. That I feed the hungry, that I forgive an insult, that I love my enemy in the name of Christ—all these are undoubtedly great virtues. What I do unto the least of my brethren, that I do unto Christ. But what if I should discover that the least amongst them all, the poorest of all the beggars, the most impudent of all the offenders, the very enemy himself—that these are within me, and that I myself stand in need of the alms of my own kindness—that I myself am the enemy who must be loved—what then? . . . Neurosis is an inner cleavage—the state of being at war with oneself. Everything that accentuates this cleavage makes the patient worse, and everything that mitigates it tends to heal the patient.

The very thing which I am so reluctant to concede to others and to myself is, in fact, our greatest need: true love and appreciation of self. Self-doubt and self-hatred are the common cancers that have so badly ravaged humanity, distorting and destroying social relationships and trust. I am sure that almost all human neuroses and moral evils stem from this one common cause: the absence of true love of one-self.

the origin of our problems

Of course it all begins in those most important years of any human life, the first two. A baby is born into this world like a living question searching for answers. Who am I? What am I worth? What is life about? What am I supposed to be and do?

The answers start coming in immediately. If a child receives an abundance of affection, hugs, kisses, lullabies, laughing and warmth, he will begin hearing optimistic and joyful answers to his questions. They will seep into him and be indelibly recorded there. He will begin to know the one thing he needs most to know: I am lovable! I don't have to do anything or be anything but myself. I am valuable and worthwhile in myself.

However, if his parents, and especially his mother with whom he presumably has most contact, are unable or unwilling to express affection, if they are cold and matter-of-fact, irritated by the baby's middle-of-the-night needs or impatient with his incontinence, the infant will in his own way absorb these facts. The non-verbal communication of this irritation, displeasure or even anger is recorded forever in the human organism of the child. Somehow the baby senses that he has caused these reactions. He is not only recording these messages but he also is recording his own emotional responses of doubt, anxiety, and insecurity. They will play back to him and in him for the rest of his life.

Later, when the baby begins to talk and listen, his impressions of himself and his worth will be deepened through verbal communication. If he hears warm words, like "I love you. . . . My Darling . . . . Good Boy. . . . Daddy's Little Girl. . . . etc." the child will know that he is good and lovable. He will begin to develop a sense of personal worth and security that will dispose him for the rest of his life to openness and friendliness with others. He will always anticipate warmth and love from others, and so be inclined to trust them and be open with them.

Most of us, to a greater or lesser degree, have heard a very different message. We were offered love, but it was always somehow "conditional" love. A baby, even in his first encounter with words, can easily hear conditions attached to his parents' love: "If you are quiet. . . . If you eat your dinner. . . . If you don't make a mess. . . . If you act like your brother or sister. . . . etc." Later, as the child develops so do these conditions of tentative love. The growing child hears a new set of stipulations for receiving love: "If you help around the house. . . . If you stay clean . . . . If you get good grades in school . . . . etc." The point is always clear whatever the conditions may be. There is a "price of admission" for love, and you've got to pay it. Your worth is not in yourself, but in something else, in your appearance, your actions, your success, in being and doing what is expected of you.

Parents tend to use this kind of manipulation by the pulling or pushing of various levers: smiles or frowns, warmth or coldness, words or silence, etc. Today we would call it "behavior modification." The desired behavior is achieved by providing rewards for compliance and penalties for failure. The price which such treatment exacts of the child can be catastrophic in terms of his own self-image and ability to love himself. A child who has been taught his lessons by having love turned on and off eventually concludes that his sole worth and goodness lie in his ability to fulfill the needs and wishes of others. In no sense does he live *for himself* but only *for others*.

The usual demands made by conditional, parental love are: compliance, cooperation, conformity, being like somebody, doing one's best always, being a success, working hard, causing no trouble, glorifying the family name, making one's parents proud, etc. Of course, when all the conditions are added up they are just too much. Under conditions like these one can only fail, and in failure be deprived of love. After all, failure means that you didn't pay the necessary price of admission to love. This, of course, leads to self-hatred, whether consciously admitted or not. And this self-hatred is the beginning of a sad and self-destructive life. Erich Fromm, in his *Art of Loving,* writes:

To be loved because of one's merit, because one deserves it, always leaves doubt; maybe I did not please the person whom I want to love me, maybe this or that—there is always a fear that love could disappear.

Furthermore, "deserved" love easily leaves a bitter feeling that one is not loved for oneself, that one is loved only because one pleases, that one is, in the last analysis, not loved at all but used.

adjustments to the painful reality

The human organism is extremely resourceful in adjusting to various situations. It has a way of compensating for losses and attempting recovery. To the extent that an infant-child has not been assured of his worth and lovability, he begins to adapt, to act and react in ways that will spare him the sharpest edge of pain and/or fill in his painful voids. Some of his devices will be designed to avoid further pain, while others will be directed to inviting and winning love. I would like to run through a brief and partial list of such devices, behavioral symptoms which appear in people who have not learned to love and esteem themselves. The severity of the symptom, the extent to which the device is employed, will always be proportionate to the greater or lesser absence of true self-love and self-esteem.

Exaggerating or bragging. By definition bragging here implies self-flattery with the intended purpose of achieving recognition and a sense of worth, both in one's own eyes and the eyes of others. As we often sense, the poor braggart is not only trying to convince us of his ability or worth, but also himself. In general he is met with unkindness. Many people volunteer for the work of putting him in his place. It is a sad reversal, because the braggart is convinced that love and recognition are conditional, and he is trying to present his credentials as the price of admission.

A critical attitude. The person who does not love himself may adapt to his condition by becoming a critic of others, always finding and pointing out their faults. Of course, his accusations are really self-accusations though he does not realize this. His criticism is based on a projection of what he thinks he is. Since hating himself for his worthlessness and faults would be too painful, he projects them into others, and proceeds to ventilate his venom with deadly aim.

Rationalization. The person without love of self has no sense of personal worth and his only assumed worth rests on his ability to perform. Consequently, when his performance leaves something to be desired he immediately excuses himself, rationalizes his failure. To admit that he is wrong, to confess his faults and failures would mean too much pain. He can never afford to lose an argument or have false information, etc. His worth is only conditional and such failures would destroy the last vestiges of self-respect.

Perfectionism. Such a person is driven to do whatever he attempts with meticulous perfection. Performance is the assumed condition for recognition and love; so his performance becomes crucially important. He is always trying to pass the test, pay the price of admission into a feeling of personal worth. To measure up to the expectations of those who can give him recognition or refuse it becomes his treadmill.

Shyness. Since he has been taught that people will accept him only on certain conditions, his basic reaction to people is fear. He fears their criticism, their evaluation of himself, their rejection in the end. To avoid running this risk, he may wall himself in, protect himself by a veil of shyness. At least in certain situations in which he cannot be confident, he feels very shy and withdrawn. It is a kind of psychological insulation against failure, and it is a serious matter since it is his person and his worth that are always on trial.

Self-depreciation. One way of adjusting to this painful condition of emptiness is to paint such a depressing picture of oneself that others will not expect much, will refrain from criticism, and maybe even extend sympathy. The portrait of a "deprived victim" will not threaten others, and so their treatment of the victim may even include an attempt to build him up.

Anger. The person afflicted by a sense of personal worthlessness first hates his own inadequacy and futility. Soon he is hating himself. When this anger is turned in on himself it takes the form of depression and despondency. It is much less painful to ventilate it on others by acting out in some temper tantrum his own very painful condition.

Defensive docility. Another possible adjustment to the absence of true self-esteem is to become a submissive observer of every regulation, law, and rule with mechanical precision. The person in question has learned very early in life that such compliance brings a reward, a smile or embrace, so he keeps trying. He attempts to be a completely good, obedient person. He feels safer this way from criticism since he can hide his real self behind rules and his observance of them. He is continually angling for approval.

Becoming a loner. Obviously, a wounded spirit reasons, it is safer not to get involved with others. They will only find out that he is not lovable in himself. They will start imposing all the same old, tiring conditions for recognition and love. It's easier just to avoid this exhausting game, to go it alone. He may play at surface sociability, but deep down he is still essentially alone.

Over-achieving. To some extent we all believe that what we *do* will make up for what we fail to *be* in ourselves. We are tempted to want the achievement of "great deeds," to own big and magnificent things, in the hopes that these will get us attention and recognition. To many people caught in this intended adjustment, achievements and possessions are construed as an extension of self, and such people need all the extensions they can get.

Masks, roles, facades. The person who has received and knows only conditional love cannot tolerate much criticism of his actions, opinions, or person. He has been hurt and wants to risk no further vulnerability. Criticism of his actions or person would undermine his whole existence. So he may seek immunity from such devastating criticism by putting some kind of an act on the stage rather than by putting himself on the line. If people criticize his act, he can always change it. If they criticize his honest person or authentic acts he would be destroyed.

Introjection. Basically dissatisfied with himself, the person who feels worthless will tend to identify with someone else, preferably a public or private hero. He will be like a little boy taking on the mannerisms of an athletic star or a little girl pretending she is a cinema queen. Both "introject" qualities and abilities which they do not have. Even this pretense is consoling.

Absolute agreeability. One of the saddest adjustments made by people who cannot love themselves is to play at being the all-time nice person. Such a person will offer his agreement on any subject at any time in order to barter for a little recognition and approval. He is not really genuine. He is sad and compromising. However, he would rather settle for absolute agreeability than the alternative of absolute loneliness.

Cynicism, suspicion. Because such a person perceives no value in himself, he also has no trust for himself. In the blind belief that everyone is really like him, he extends and projects his own self-distrust. He believes in and trusts no one.

Timidity. Unlike shyness, which concerns reluctance with respect to personal relationships, timidity refers to a reluctance to venture, to undertake new projects. Afraid to love and afraid to be loved because of the danger of ultimate failure and rejection, the person without a sense of personal worth will be afraid to attempt anything of significance. He is, in fact, cut off from much of reality by his fear. He will not try the new because he might be wrong. He fears to express himself because he might make a mistake or someone might challenge him. He fears making overtures to others because they might dislike him.

summary

Everyone is born with unique and unconditional value. Each of us is mysterious and unrepeatable in the whole course of human history, made after the image and likeness of God himself. But we can know ourselves only as reflected in the eyes of others. Consequently, our basic endowment of self-appreciation is largely the gift of our parents. However, if we have perceived from them—as all of us have to some extent—that their love for us was only conditional, that it was turned on only when we met their conditions and turned off when we failed to meet them, that their love was not based on what we are but conditioned on our performance, we can only conclude that our value is somehow outside ourselves. There is no cause within for true self-love, self-esteem, self-appreciation. There is no occasion for celebration.

When worthiness of love becomes a matter of passing tests and fulfilling conditions, we begin to experience more failure than success. In the experience of repeated failure, there is conflict, fear, frustration, pain, and ultimately some form of self-hatred. So we spend the rest of our lives trying to escape this pain through one of the devices described above. Or we try to assume an appearance that will please others and gain us loving acceptance. We give up on being ourselves and try to be someone else, someone who will be worthy of recognition and love.

what does it mean to love yourself?

When I was young and very zealous I once told an older and wiser man that I was going to spend all my life and all my energies loving others. He gently asked if I was going to love myself with equal determination. I protested that loving others would leave no time for loving myself. It sounded very saintly. However, my older and wiser friend looked at me long and pensively. Finally he said, "You are on a suicide course." My facile reply was: "What a nice way to go, eh?" But, of course, he was right. I now know what he knew all the time: true love of others is premised on a true love of oneself.

To understand what it means to love oneself, let us first ask what it means to love another. In the following chapter I would like to investigate the deeper meanings and implications of love. For now let us say only that love does at least these three things:

1 Love esteems and affirms the unconditional and unique value of the one loved.
2 Love acknowledges and tries to fulfill the needs of the one loved.
3 Love forgives and forgets the failings of the one loved.

When we are asked to "love our neighbor as ourselves," the clear implication is that whatever we would do for our neighbor we would *also and first* do for ourselves. In other words, it's a package deal. You have two people you must love: yourself and your neighbor. You can't really love one without loving the other.

To understand how this would work in actual practice, it might help to imagine yourself as somehow another person, whom you must truly love. Stand off at a distance, and ask yourself: Have you really tried to see and affirm his (your) unconditional and unique value? Do you really try to consider and fulfill his (your) needs? Have you really forgiven him (yourself) for his faults and mistakes? Think about it. Do you think of him as gently and lovingly as you do those others in your life whom you love most? Do you offer him the same kind of warmth and understanding as you offer them?

One final example. Let us say that someone else asks you a favor. Now love asks you to try to fulfill your friend's need, but there is also someone else that you must consider with equal attention: yourself. Let us look at your needs. One of your primary needs is to go out in love to others. The only way to be loved is to be loving. The only truly happy people are those who have found someone, some cause to

In other words, it's a package deal.
You have two people you must love:
yourself and your neighbor.

love and belong to. However, you may have other needs to be considered. You may need rest, or you may have another pressing duty, etc. It may be that, all things considered, you will have to refuse your friend's request.

What I am describing is not self-preoccupation or narcissism. It is simply a description of a balanced love, extended with the same concern to self and to neighbor. The balance can shift, so that we give all our concern only to self or attempt to give all our concern only to our neighbor. But neither of these attitudes is humanly viable. Neither is true love.

the gospel of Glasser

Whether this basic human need be described as self-love, self-esteem, self-appreciation, or self-celebration (each seems to bring out a different facet), one thing is sure. This need cannot be seriously frustrated without a general breakdown of the whole personality. Dr. William Glasser, author of *Reality Therapy* and one of the bright and innovative psychiatrists of our day, makes two fundamental assumptions about this sense of personal worth. I am sure that he is correct.

The first assumption is that *all* psychological problems, from the slightest neuroses to the deepest psychoses, are symptomatic of the frustration of this fundamental human need for a sense of personal worth. The depth and duration of the symptomatic problem (phobias, guilt complexes, paranoia, etc.) are only indicative of the depth and duration of the deprivation of self-esteem.

Glasser's second assumption is that the self-image of any human being will be the radical determining factor of all his behavior. True and realistic self-esteem is the basic element in the health of any human personality. People act, and especially relate to other people, in accordance with the way they think of and feel about themselves.

Theoretical assent to these assumptions and to the basic necessity of self-esteem may not be too difficult. However, practical acknowledgement in the dust of daily battle can be an heroic achievement. I can easily trace your obnoxious behavior to the invisible roots of an unsuccessful struggle for self-esteem, until you hurt me. Then my own psychological scars begin to ache, and I stop thinking about you and your needs. I stop trying to understand you and I am tempted to judge you and even to hurt you. I must tell you this. It is very important that you know it. I want to offer you unconditional love. I really know you need it and I want to fulfill your needs so that you may be fully alive. But I am not able to do this. I am not able to give you the unconditional love you need. My own needs are too real, too limiting, too crippling. I can only say that I will do what I can. I can only ask you to be patient with me.

But I want you to know that I do know what you need, even when I cannot give it to you. My own limitations and weakness will impede my performance, but I know that my greatest contribution to your life will be to help you love yourself, to think better and more gently of yourself, to accept your own limitations more peacefully in the perspective of your whole person, which is uniquely valuable. To give you all that you need would require a wholeness in me that I do not have. I cannot always come through for you as you need me to. I am living at the outer rim of my own ideals, hanging on only with great effort. But I can promise you this much. I will try. I will try always to reflect to you your unique and unrepeatable value and worth. I will try to be a mirror

31

to your beauty and goodness. I will try to read your heart, not your lips. I will always try to understand you rather than judge you. I will never demand that you meet my expectations as the price of admission to my heart.

So do not ask me *why* I love you. Such a question could invite only the response of conditional love. I do not love you because you look a certain way or do certain things or practice certain virtues. Only ask me this: "*Do* you love me?" That I can answer: "Yes, oh yes."

the options

It is our thesis that a human being will find a satisfying life in proportion to his esteem for and belief in himself. It would be wonderful if we could simply make a once-for-all decision to love and believe in ourselves. Such habitual self-confidence would free us from all the parasites which deprive us of 90% of our human life-potential. But this is clearly impossible. Everybody agrees. We cannot make it alone. I need your love and you need mine. I need to see my worth and beauty in the reflection of your eyes, in the sound of your voice, in the touch of your hand. And you need to see your worth mirrored back to you by me in the same way. We can succeed or fail together, but separate and alone we can only fail.

People without a sense of self-appreciation can only suffer, and when one hurts with this pain, he hurts twenty-four uninterrupted hours a day. We can handle pains that are self-limiting, like headaches or sunburn. We know they will eventually go away. But how can we handle the pain of failure that strikes at the very center of our being and existence? When will this go away?

The only truly happy people
are those who have found someone,
some cause to love and belong to.

To complicate this most fundamental of all human problems is the fact that love from others, which is the radical source of self-esteem, cannot be banked as money can. Self-esteem fluctuates. We cannot glom on to yesterday's sources of self-celebration and coast along on them for the rest of life. There must be a constant intake of reassurance from the love of others. When we find ourselves without love and without recognition of our own worth, we feel empty, bankrupt. We hurt and we hurt very deep down. We are aware of hurting, but this pain, unlike many other pains, doesn't tell us what we must do. When I touch a very hot object, the pain tells me to pull away quickly. But the pain of self-hatred and worthlessness is too diffuse, harder to understand and interpret. There is no simple "set of directions" built into this pain.

Most people seek relief by distraction, living like barnacles on the TV screen or dissolving themselves in work or play. But distraction is not solution. It can only be temporary. It only forestalls the eventual foreclosure of pain. So people who have failed to find satisfaction and peace within themselves usually resort to one of four rather permanent options. In outlining these options, Dr. Glasser insists that each represents an attempted escape from the pain of failure as a person. To the extent that we fail to perceive worth in ourselves, we will retreat into one of these analgesic shelters.

1 Depression. While psychological depression is an emotional state of morbid dejection and sadness, ranging from mild discouragement to utter despair, it can be and is used as a surrogate or substitute form of suffering. When a human psychological motor is vibrating with a dangerously violent pain, depression is an idling, a slowing down of the motor. It saves the motor from breaking apart. Depression spares the person from the agony of his

34

deeper pain, protects him from the full impact of his unbearable life situation.

It is useless to suggest to people who have sought the refuge of this option that they "cheer up." Subconsciously at least they must reject such a suggestion. If they were to give up their depression and then find no sense of personal worth, they would be thrown back into the scourging pain of personal failure, from which the depression was an attempted escape. The depression was an alternative in desperation, an option, a protection from the shattering, unbearable fact of personal worthlessness.

It was recently reported in midwestern newspapers that a young husband and father, piloting his own plane and taking his family on vacation, lost his way and the plane crashed. The man himself was the only survivor. All the others were killed. The poor man proceeded to arrange the funerals of his loved ones, and, when everything was completed, he calmly killed himself. Friends said that he had shown no signs of deep depression. He seemed to be brave and composed in his moment of grief. The fact of the matter is that, if he had been deeply depressed, he probably would not have killed himself. Contrary to what is usually thought, terribly depressed people do not kill themselves. The depression defuses the violence of the emotions that often lead to self-destruction.

2 Anger and antisocial behavior. The second option is anger. When we choose this alternative, we "act out" the bitter sense of failure and frustration that accompany a sense of worthlessness. Anger is almost always the result of a deeper fear and hidden insecurity. When we feel unsuccessful as persons, we can opt to ventilate this pain through antisocial behavior. If the pain is deep enough, we may even kill, but certainly we will be the cause of some kind of trouble. We will find some way to make the lives of others miserable.

Like depression, "acting out in anger" is designed to be a release from the deeper pain of personal failure. The angry, abusive behavior is a veiled expression of frustration, fear and self-rejection. This kind of "acting out" is often used in psychotherapy. People are encouraged, in some form of psychodrama, to act out their repressed feelings under controlled circumstances and conditions.

3 Insanity. When failure to find love and a sense of worth in the real world becomes too painful, rather than try to change ourselves, we may opt to change the world. We can "make up" our own world, inside ourselves, and retreat into that world. Insanity is essentially a loss of contact with reality. The condition of being "split from" reality (schizophrenia) may be regarded not as a disease in itself, but as a subconsciously adopted method of thinking, feeling, and acting which creates a new and personal world, in which one will not have to cope with the problem of personal failure. In this sense insanity is really a choice and much like the retreat into fantasy used by children in their traumatic moments of disappointment. Insanity is both a choice and an escape, a liberation from a very uncomfortable world and life.

4 Physical sickness. Dr. Glasser, with most physicians, believes that the most commonly chosen of all the options is physical sickness. In taking this course the psychological pain of failure is translated into physical symptoms, which are usually much easier to bear. Many sicknesses formerly considered to be organic are coming to be viewed as "psychosomatic" because psychological factors have been found to be so significant in their origin.

Physical illness is easier to bear than the failure to find personal worth because there is less awareness of disgrace and culpability associated with physical sickness. It is easier to say that I have an ulcer than to admit my worthlessness as a person. Also, there is probably involved in this option a throwback to childhood. As children our physical pains and sicknesses usually evoked more sympathy than our personal unhappiness. A scratched knee got more loving attention than a wounded spirit.

At any rate, it is commonly estimated that 90-95% of all physical illness is psychologically induced. Even such "objective" illnesses as viral or bacterial infections can be psychologically aided and abetted. Tensions and frustrations lower the immunization and resistance mechanisms of the body, opening the doors to sickness. No doubt, too, autosuggestion is involved. It is easier to admit a physical pain than a personal failure.

Dr. Glasser tells an interesting story of a psychotic patient whom he visited on his daily rounds as a psychiatrist in a mental hospital. One day a man who had previously been completely disoriented seemed suddenly to have come back into contact with reality. He looked up at Dr. Glasser and very calmly and deliberately announced that he was sick. Upon examination it turned out that the man actually did have pneumonia. During the period of convalescence from pneumonia all symptoms of insanity disappeared. Only gradually, after recovering completely from the pneumonia, did the symptoms of insanity recur. Glasser's surprising explanation: the man had briefly changed the option by which he was assuaging his personal pain. He had moved from insanity to physical sickness and back again to insanity.

the addictions

Each of the options described above is an alternative to the admission of failure as a person. However, while each of these options somehow camouflages and alleviates the essential agony, there is still pain. People still hurt, and so, as Glasser points out, they may well turn to some form of pain-killing addiction in addition to the original escape-option. Alcohol and opium are the most effective pain-killers, though they are addictive and destructive. Some people choose a negative or destructive form of addiction, like dope or alcohol. Others choose a neutral addiction like food. Still others choose a form of addiction that is generally considered positive, like work. So we have, among other victims of addiction, alcoholics, foodaholics and workaholics. The one thing that they all have in common is that they are trying to dull the pain of a seemingly worthless existence.

The self-defeating part of all forms of addiction is that, if one succeeds and does remove the pain, the tranquilized sufferer no longer has the needed impetus to seek and find his own worth as a person. He tends to withdraw from life. One of the most frightening tragedies of our times is the addiction of enormous numbers of people to drugs, many of which have been proclaimed biogenetically destructive. The saddest part of the tragedy is that, once a person gets into drugs, he has crossed a bridge into a world of unreality, and he has burned that bridge behind him. Once he lives in unreality he can no longer recognize reality, see things as they really are, hear them as they really are, cope with them as they really are.

Consequently, eminent psychiatrists, such as Viktor Frankl, object to the use of all "high" producing drugs, including marijuana, on the grounds that addicts and even potheads eventually lose the ability to distinguish between reality and illusion, between the facts and their fantasies. Sadly, too, once an addiction has begun to rule its victim, the addict prefers his addiction to everything and everyone else.

conclusion

Pain in itself is not an evil to be avoided at all costs. Pain is rather a teacher from whom we can learn much. Pain is instructing us, telling us to change, to stop doing one thing or to begin doing another, to stop thinking one way and begin thinking differently. When we refuse to listen to pain and its lessons, all we have left is one of the escapist tendencies of the options and addictions. In effect we have said: I will not listen. I will not learn. I will not change.

When applied to human beings almost all labels are meaningless. However, I do think that there is one really meaningful distinction, and that is between "growing" and "static-escapist" people. It is a distinction between those who are "open" to growth and those who are "closed." Open and growing people do not begrudge the pedagogy of pain, and are willing to try change. They will initiate appropriate responses and adjustments. Others, for reasons we do not know, simply will not address themselves to the lessons of pain. They rather seek a narcotized and tranquilized existence, a peace without profit. They are willing to settle for 10% of their potential. They are willing to die without having really lived.

There is something that a growing person can do, a way to find personal worth, self-esteem, self-appreciation, and a cause to celebrate. We will take this up in the following chapter. Through true and lasting love, we can recover acceptance of self, a realization of our worth. When these are present, everything else will somehow move in the direction of growth on the paths of peace. When love and worth are missing, there is left only a partial existence. We can achieve only a fraction of what might have been. We will die without having really lived. The glory of God—a man fully alive—will forever be diminished.

Pain is
a teacher
from whom
we can
learn much.

CHAPTER TWO

A thought transfixed me: For the first time in my life I saw the truth as it is set into song by so many poets, proclaimed as the final wisdom by so many thinkers. The truth—that love is the ultimate and highest goal to which man can aspire. Then I grasped the meaning of the greatest secret that human poetry and human thought and belief have to impart: the salvation of man is through love and in love.

Viktor Frankl, *Man's Search for Meaning*

human needs and the experience of love

salvation in and through love

Most people are never able to achieve the fullness of life that represents the highest glory of God in man. They remain forever shackled by doubts, fears, and guilt, trading in pain-dulling options and addictions. The world of advertising plays upon the tortured spirit of man, promising him treats in taste, blue vacation skies, better mattresses, etc. He buys these things, hoping to fly now and pay later, until the closets of his life become cluttered. But the pain goes on.

Profound change never comes quickly or easily. Modification in habits of behavior, a revision in basic attitudes and life orientation, unknotting old prejudices and running the risk of openness—this is a wide, round curve that can be negotiated only slowly, not a sharp corner that can be turned all at once.

But one thing is clear. All psychological research has established this fact beyond doubt. More important than any psychological theory, teaching, or therapeutic technique, that which heals and promotes human change and growth is a one-to-one relationship of love.

the anatomy
of effective love

What is this love that works the miracle of human healing and liberation? Somehow, I think, we know instinctively what love means, both when we are loving and when we are loved. However, it will help to talk more specifically about the nature of love. For a working definition, I would like to use the description of love given by Dr. Harry Stack Sullivan in *Conceptions of Modern Psychiatry:*

When the satisfaction, security and development of another person become as significant to you as your own satisfaction, security and development, love exists.

In theory, love implies a basic attitude of concern for the satisfaction, security and development of the one loved. In practice, love implies that I am ready and willing to forego my own convenience, to invest my own time, and even to risk my own security to promote your satisfaction, security and development. If I have the basic attitude of love and I am

44

That which heals
and promotes
human change
and growth
is a one-to-one
relationship of love.

able to translate it into action, the presumption is that I love you. But this is only a working definition of love. There are, in the complicated anatomy of love, many other theses which must be duly acknowledged.

thesis one:
love is not a feeling

I feel pretty sure that most of the people I know identify love with a feeling or emotion. They "fall in love" and they "fall out of love," in uneven rhythms. The flame of love is extinguished in their lives only until a new match can be struck. I remember a young lady telling me that her husband announced at the end of their honeymoon that he no longer loved her. It was only two weeks after I had witnessed their marriage vows, and so I figured that something was wrong with him or his idea of love either then or now.

Now, everyone knows that feelings are like yo-yos, up and down, depending on such fickle things as the barometer, amounts of sunshine, digestion, the time of the month and the side of the bed out of which we crawl on a given morning. Feelings are fickle, and people who identify love with feelings become fickle lovers. The French novelist, Anatole France, once wrote that "In love only the beginnings are delightful. That is why we keep beginning again, falling in love all over again." When we identify love with feelings, we go through life searching for "that old feeling" which crooners have immortalized in song.

It is obvious that feelings *are related to love*. The first attraction of love is usually experienced in terms of very strong feelings. And I cannot—unless I am some kind of hero or masochist—put your satisfaction, security and development on a par with my own if I do not for the most part have supportive, loving feelings towards you. However, in the course of a love-relationship, we will have to go through an occasional winter of emotional discontent to find a newness of our love in the springtime. As the tinsel of young love is burnished by time into the more valuable gold of mature love, there will be times when emotional satisfaction will be absent, and there will be other times when negative feelings will cloud the skies of our world; but certainly growth in love supposes and needs generally good emotional weather.

It would be fatal to identify love with a feeling, because of the fickleness of feelings. However, it would be equally lethal to a relationship of love if there were no warm and loving feelings to support the intentions of love.

thesis two:
love is
a decision-commitment

In this chapter, we are considering the interpersonal relationship of love. Such a relationship admits of many levels. I can love and be loved by another as my father or mother, brother or sister, close friend, closest friend and total confidant, husband or wife. The contract of love would be different in each of these cases. Obviously, I cannot have a deep, sharing relationship with many people. There is not enough time, nor do I have the emotional capacity to interact in a deeply personal and loving way with many people. Erich Fromm writes:

Love is an activity, not a passive affect; it is a "standing in," not a "falling for." In the most general way, the active character of love can be described by stating that love is primarily *giving*, not receiving.

I cannot enter into a love-relationship with many people. I would be exhausted in the effort. So I must choose. Of course, there will be certain reciprocal obligations and responsibilities between myself and those to whom I am related by bloodlines, but even here there is room for choice. I can freely and legitimately choose my father or my mother to be my special confidant, one of my brothers or sisters as my special friend. The greatest gift that I have to give to another is my love, and I must carefully choose those in whom I will invest this sacred capacity.

How do I make this decision? All sorts of considerations enter into such decision making, from the amount of things I can share in common with another, our capacity to fulfill each other's needs, temperament, interests, intelligence, values, artistic and athletic abilities, physical appearance, right down to that mysterious thing called "chemistry." So I look around at those who are in my world, and make my choices, and offer my love accordingly. There may be somewhere in this universe someone who would be just right for me, tailor-made to all my preferences, but that person may not be in my immediate world, the world from which I must choose those whom I will love.

Since love can exist on many levels, it is extremely important not to offer a commitment of love which I may not be able to honor. Inexperienced and immature people tend to do this, to say things under the impulse of strong emotions or physical reactions (and under the trees at night), which have a hollow sound the next morning after coffee.

Immature people say things
under the impulse of strong emotions
which have a hollow sound
the next morning after coffee.

The danger of such a premature, undeliberated commitment is this. Most people lurk behind protective walls, what Harry Stack Sullivan calls "security operations." These are designed to protect an already injured ego from further vulnerability. At the call of love, these people come out, perhaps haltingly at first, but they do come out, reassured by the promises of love. If I have made a premature or overstated commitment, I will later have to take back my promises made to such a person. I will have to explain that I really did not mean what I said, or that I have changed my mind. I will leave that person standing painfully naked and unprotected. He will return again to the forests of a new security operation, go back behind a higher and more impenetrable wall. And, once burned, doubly cautious, it may be a long time before anyone will ever successfully call him out again, if that be possible at all. The person who has experienced only a fragile, conditional, and temporary kind of love will no doubt find the adventure of human life very painful and precarious.

Such care and consideration in making the commitment of love does not, of course, preclude the fact that a young man or woman in search of a marriage partner may well try many relationships before finding the one on which he is ready to make his "life-wager." Getting to know many people, "dating" many before making the final choice and commitment is obviously a wise procedure. The caution against overstatement of intentions and a premature commitment remains valid, however, especially during this period of experimentation. The old ballad, "It's a Sin to Tell a Lie," reminds us of the many broken hearts and broken lives ". . . just because those words (I love you) were spoken."

thesis three:
effective love is unconditional

Love may be given either conditionally or un-conditionally. There is no other possibility. Either I attach conditions to my love or I do not. I would like to say at this point that only unconditional love can effect change in the life of the person to whom that love is offered.

In his work, *Conceptions of Modern Psychiatry,* from which we took our working definition of love, Dr. Sullivan talks of the "quiet miracle of developing the capacity of love." He describes being loved as the source of this miracle. The first impulse to change, he says, comes not so much from being challenged as from being loved. Only in an atmosphere of unconditionally offered love will the human barriers to relationships be lowered.

There is a story of a housewife who related that her husband's love seemed to be conditioned on her keeping the house tidy and in order at all times. She maintained that she needed to know that he loved her whether the house was cleaned up or not, in order to have the strength to keep the house clean. If you understand and agree with what she is saying, you understand the point being made here. The only kind of love that helps us change and grow is unconditional.

Conditional love always degenerates into pan-scale love. Both parties are expected, in pan-scale love, to put a donation into the proper pan so that a perfect balance is achieved. But sooner or later some tension, some pain, some struggle will distract one of the pan-scale lovers, and he will not make his monthly payment on time. So conditional lover #2, refusing to be swindled, removes part of his contribution in order to be sure that more isn't going out than coming in—until nothing is left but emotional or legal divorce.

There is another question, and it is not so simple. Can we expect one party in a love relationship to continue making an unconditional contribution and commitment of love without a sustaining response from the other? Theoretically, I believe that if a person could continue offering an unconditional love, the other would in time respond. But perhaps it would be too late. If the person trying to offer unconditional love is given nothing in response, to nourish his own capacity and renew his strength for love, the relationship may be brought to an inevitable failure.

In practice I think this possibility is claimed far more than it actually occurs. People renege on their love commitments, run off to divorce courts, and take to falling in love all over again (with somebody else), without ever challenging their personal resources, developing their ingenuity, or testing their coping mechanisms. It has been said that love works if we will work at it. I think that this is true, and I think that fidelity will always be the measure and test of human love.

Footnote: "Unconditional love" should be interpreted as an ideal, a goal towards which true love aspires, but which is realistically not within human reach or attainment. We are all to some extent injured, limited by the throb of our own needs and pains. Only a totally unscarred and free person could consistently give unconditional love. Such a person, of course, does not exist.

thesis four: love is forever

This thesis is simply a corollary of the previous thesis. A time limit on love is only one of the conditions we can attach to our commitment. I will love you as long as, until. . . . In the movie, *Butterflies Are*

Free, the superficial, scatterbrained nymphet played so well by Goldie Hawn is portrayed in the act of running away from her blind lover. She explains her flight: ". . . because you are blind. You're crippled!" In the most profound moment of the movie, the young man replies: "No, I am not crippled. I am sightless but not crippled. You are crippled, because you can't commit yourself to anyone. You can't belong."

The commitment of love, at whatever level, has to be a permanent thing, a life-wager. If I say that I am your friend, I will always be your friend, not as long as or until anything. I will always be there for you. Effective love is not like the retractable point on a ballpoint pen. If I say I am your man, I will always be your man. In the words of another old song, "When I fall in love, it will be forever."

Any other kind of love loses its effect. I need to know that the love you offer me is a permanent offer before I will give up my security operations, my masks, roles and games. I cannot come out to a temporary, tentative love, to an offer which has all that fine print and many footnotes in the contract.

thesis five:
the commitment of love involves:
decisions . . .
decisions . . .
decisions . . .

We have said that love is a commitment to the satisfaction, security and development of the one loved. In loving you I am committed to the fulfillment of your needs, whatever they may be. But there is a double difficulty here (I didn't promise you a rose garden!): First of all, your needs are constantly changing. If I love you, I have to be constantly reading your needs, watching you with the look of love. I must be asking: What do you need me to be today, this morning, tonight? Are you discouraged and in need of my strength? Have you experienced some success and are you inviting me to rejoice, to celebrate with you? Or are you lonely and need only my hand softly in yours? This kind of empathetic listening and looking is one of the deepest challenges of effective love. It is not easy to know who you are at any given moment and what you may need me to be.

The second difficulty involved in the practice of love is this. It is I, not you, who must decide what you need me to be. I cannot simply ask you and trust you to know. It may well be that, according to my lights, the most loving thing for me to do is to tell you a truth which you do not want to hear, or to stay by your side even when you are angrily telling me to go away, or to resurrect an unsettled discussion which you want to abandon in disgust. In taking on the responsibility for these decisions, I will be right sometimes and I will be wrong sometimes, but more important than the rightness or wrongness of my judgments will always be the fact that I did what I did because I loved you. I wanted what was best for you. I chose to feel responsible for your life, growth and the development of all your human powers.

Of course, my decisions must never in any way preempt your freedom. I must be me and offer my gift, but at the same time I must let you be you, free to accept or to reject my gift. This is perhaps the most difficult line that true love must walk, being myself and offering my contributions according to my lights and yet never forcing your acceptance or response.

thesis six:
the essential gift of love
is a sense of personal worth

If what we have said in chapter one, that the ability to feel good about one's self, to love, appreciate and celebrate one's own goodness is the key factor in the health of human personality and the basic ingredient of human happiness, then the essential contribution of love is clear. My love must empower you to love yourself. We should judge our success in loving not by those who admire us for our accomplishments, but by the number of those who attribute their wholeness to our loving them, by the number of those who have seen their beauty in our eyes, heard their goodness acknowledged in the warmth of our voices. We are like mirrors to one another. No one can know what he looks like until he sees his reflection in some kind of mirror. It is an absolute human certainty that no one can know his own beauty or perceive a sense of his own worth until it has been reflected back to him in the mirror of another loving, caring human being.

thesis seven:
love means the affirmation,
not the possession of the one loved

A sense of his own worth is no doubt the greatest gift we can offer to another, the greatest contribution we can make to any life. We can give this gift and make this contribution only through love. However, it is essential that our love be liberating, not possessive. We must at all times give those we love the freedom to be themselves. Love affirms the other *as*

55

other. It does not possess and manipulate him *as mine.* Pertinent here is the quotation of Frederick Perls: "You did not come into this world to live up to my expectations. And I did not come into the world to live up to yours. If we meet it will be beautiful. If we don't, it can't be helped."

In Old English the word for love is *frēon,* from which the word *friend* is derived. To love is to liberate. Even in the structure of the language there is an implication that love and friendship are freeing. Love and friendship must empower those we love to become their best selves, according to their own lights and visions.

This means that wanting what is best for you and trying to be what you need me to be can be done only in a way that preserves your freedom to have your own feelings, think your own thoughts, and make your own decisions. If your personhood is as dear to me as my own, which is the implication of love, I must respect it carefully and sensitively. When I affirm you, my affirmation is based on your unconditional value as an unique, unrepeatable and even sacred mystery of humanity.

In evaluating my love for you, I must then address myself to the question of whether my love is in fact possessive and manipulative or really affirming and freeing. It will help, in this evaluation, to ask myself these questions: Is it more important to me that you be pleased with yourself or that I be pleased with you? Is it more important that you attain the goals you have set for yourself, or that you attain the goals I want for you?

Another test is this: to the extent that I truly love and affirm you, you will be enabled to relate more successfully to other people, and I will rejoice in this. I will want you to love others and others to love

Conditional love always degenerates into pan-scale love.

you. I will not want to become "your whole life." A person "fully alive" will relate well to many people and enjoy a great variety of things. My love must affirm and free you to live fully, to be alive in all your parts and powers, to experience fully the range of heavenly glory that fills our world.

the dynamics of love

So far we have said that the essential factor in human personality adjustment and the wellspring of the fullness of life is true appreciation and celebration of oneself. Where this is present, peace and joy will abound. Where this is absent, there will be sad attempts to escape into options and addictions in an effort to dull the edge of pain. Consequently, if we truly love another and want his satisfaction, security and development, this sense of personal worth will be the chief contribution we can make to the person loved and to the fullness of his life. After having defined the nature and function of love, we would like to investigate now the dynamics of love, the process and experience which alone can result in a secure self-image, an abiding sense of personal worth and the consequent joy that will fill the whole of a human life.

The very nature of man is dialogical. Human life is a basic relatedness. The I of one is in constant search of the Thou of another and the We of a love-relationship. The success or failure of this search is the essential success or failure of a human life. To be human is to love and to be loved. The basic cause of all mental and emotional illness is the inability to form deep, human relationships of love.

The innate need to be loved is revealed in the earliest moments of infancy. The feeling of being wanted and the satisfaction of belonging are absolute requirements from the very moment a person is born into this world. There is a universal agreement that the amount of affection received in infancy determines, more than any other influence, the whole course and quality of a human life. Dr. Lee Salk is a pediatric psychologist. In his recent book, *What Every Child Would Like His Parents To Know,* he summarizes and presents the evidence and argument that our physical and psychological welfare is very largely a product of affectionate, demonstrative love received in infancy.

Later, during childhood, many youngsters are bothered by the fantasy that they are not wanted and will even play games to get reassurance. Temper tantrums, threats to run away from home, antisocial behavior, etc. are all thinly veiled appeals for that basic knowledge so essential to human life: a sense of personal worth as recognized only in being loved. Parents should, in every way possible, assure children of their worth and their lovability. Only when the child knows that he is *loved* can he get to that necessary truth about himself, that he is *lovable*. And only when he really believes that he is lovable will he then anticipate and expect friendliness and love from others during the course of his life. It is in this secure condition and expectation that a person is enabled to go out lovingly and trustingly to others, to run the risks of loving and being loved.

If a child is not sufficiently assured, he will of course doubt his own lovability and consequently be doubtful about the reception he will get from others. It is inevitable that such insecurity will lead to defensive, self-protective games, to what Dr. Sullivan calls "security operations." The call to human relatedness, to encounters of love, so deeply implanted in the dialogical nature of man, will be frustrated in such a life. And the very buffers set up to protect the aching ego from further damage will also prevent the actual human contact and interaction of love.

After a hopefully liberating assurance from his family during childhood, a child will in the early school years seek companions of the same sex with whom he will test his new-found capacity for making friends. But the most important kind of love which promotes human maturity and wholeness will open to him at the onset of adolescence: friendship with a person of the opposite sex. The word sex is from a Latin verb *secare* which means "to cut." The implication is that God, having made human nature, cut it in half, into male and female. The whole personalist theory of heterosexuality implies that neither half can be whole without somehow being joined to the other half. e. e. cummings writes: "one's not half two. it's two are halves of one." For any individual to actualize his potential as a human being, he must have the experience of true and deep friendship with a person of the opposite sex. While this does not imply genital sexual experience, there is really no such thing as a "purely platonic" relationship in any real friendship between a man and a woman, from adolescence onward. In every such relationship sex will always be a strong element and force, either consciously or subconsciously.

Observing the proper precautions where and when needed, we should accept this sexual drive as a healthy and wholesome force which leads to a deeper actualization of the whole human personality and the capacity for life. The sex drive—and

Effective love
is not like the
retractable
point on a
ballpoint
pen.

again I am referring to general not genital sexuality—offers a new vitality, a new quality to relatedness. This is something we have all experienced in the presence of a person of the opposite sex. A new part of us seems to come alive, and it is a fact that something has been awakened and enlivened in us.

Depth psychologists, following Carl Jung, tell us that there is a male *(animus)* and a female *(anima)* component or function in every human personality. To be a fully alive or "individuated" (Jung's term) human being, both components must be brought into conscious harmony. In the normal man, due to the learned behavior of our present culture, the male component is conscious but the female unconscious. The reverse is true for a woman.

The male component or sexual function of the soul engages predominately in things of the head and will: order, logic, power, courage, protection, dependability. The female component is associated wth the things of the heart: the appreciation of art, music, religion, nature, flowers. Its main endowments are what we think of as "feminine" qualities.

It is obvious that the more both components are awakened and developed in any given individual, the more fully alive he will be and the more fully he will experience all that is good, real and beautiful in the world. Depth psychologists assure us that this awakening of the female component in a man and the male component in a woman, so essential to human wholeness, can take place only in a relationship of love with a person of the opposite sex.

A person of the opposite sex more easily calls me out of the protection of my security operations and my endless preoccupation with self, and introduces me to the possibilities of a relationship of real caring. I feel more secure with a person of the opposite sex in one respect at least, that the other is not so obviously my competitor or an object of comparison. It is consequently easier for me to confide in a person of the opposite sex, to admit my hiddenness, to risk transparency.

the counterfeits
of love

Love between a man and woman can and should be the most liberating, maturing and fulfilling experience of adult human life. However, the kind of profound union from which such blessings come is not an easy achievement. The Spanish existentialist philosopher Ortega y Gasset describes three different counterfeit versions of this love that can exist between man and woman. The counterfeit versions distort rather than develop human personality.

1 The physical conquest. In the first counterfeit of love, one or both of the partners sees the other primarily as a source of physical, sexual pleasure. The details and concessions of the whole relationship are all arranged to maximize the possibilities and opportunities for physical gratification. The partner is "used," perhaps even willingly and without deception, as a source of bodily pleasure, and, whatever protests to the contrary are raised, the partner is viewed only as a thing, an object, a condition and source of self-gratification.

2 The psychological conquest. This second delusory fiction of love is more vicious and perverse than the first counterfeit of love. The goal here is psychological conquest. The bright lines and the right moves are here more subtle, designed to seduce the partner psychologically, to get him or her to fall in love, to fall at the feet of the conqueror, to be dominated and submissive not just as a body but as a person. When this strategy succeeds, the supposed "lover" almost immediately loses interest in the other who has been won over. He or she becomes just one more mounted trophy in the game room of the mind. "When the fish is in the boat, the fun is all over."

3 The projected image. Usually, when a man and woman first "fall in love," it is not with the reality of the other person but with a "projection" of what a loved one should be. It may be that the projected image is derived from a mother or father or a dream. Carl Jung says that "every man carries his Eve in himself," meaning that every man carries in his subconscious the image of what a lovable woman is. Likewise, of course, every Eve carries her Adam within herself. This explains why certain men "fall for" certain types of women, and vice versa. The image projected may, in some cases, have very little relationship to the real person. The problem with this is that if the person insists on keeping the image and making the other conform to it, he will love only an image, only a projection. He will not even get to know the other person.

genuine love

Two Solitudes that protect, touch and greet each other. Here we find the only reality worthy of the name love. The two partners drop, however gradually, the projected image which was the first source of attraction to find the even more beautiful reality of the person. They are willing to acknowledge and respect *otherness* in each other. Each person values and tries to promote the inner vision and mysterious destiny of the other. Each counts it his privilege to assist in the growth and realization of

Answering the call to love
demands much courage
and determination
because self-exposure
always involves a risk
of being seriously hurt.

the other's vision and destiny. Rilke's brilliant poetic insight seems to capture the nature of the true love relationship:

Love is . . . a high inducement to the individual to ripen, to become something in himself, to become world, to become world to himself for another's sake. It is a great, an exorbitant demand upon him, something that chooses him out and calls him to vast things. Love consists in this, that two solitudes protect and touch and greet each other.

conclusion

When the encounter and relationship of true love are missing in a human life, it is usually because the person has either selfishly or timidly kept the doors of his heart locked and barricaded. He is either unable or unwilling to risk transparency, to expose the most sensitive areas of his soul to another. Without such willingness to risk, human life can be only a prolonged pain of starvation and the whole world only a bleak prison. Answering the call to love demands much courage and determination because self-exposure always involves a risk of being seriously hurt. But without transparency love is impossible, and without love, human life is seriously incomplete.

When a person takes the risk of loving, his love will usually be returned. Those who are willing to love will eventually find love. And then the mirror will be there, the mirror reflecting back the image of a loving person, and this is the beginning of true self-esteem and self-celebration. This is why Viktor Frankl says that the origin of true self-esteem is in "the reflected appraisal of those whom we have loved."

It has been well said that the *second hardest* thing in all the world is to engage in the challenging process of living intimately and growing with another. The *hardest* thing in all the world is to live alone. If love is anything it is a gradual process, the long round curve that must be carefully negotiated, not the sharp right angle turn that is made in an instant, once and for all. A man or woman must set out upon a long journey and walk many miles to find the joys of love. They will have to pass through deep and dark forests and there will be many dangers. They will have to be careful of love as they are of few other things. Love will demand abstinence from all that might prove poisonous to love. Love will demand much courage, perseverance and self-discipline.

But the journey to love is the journey to the fullness of life, for it is only in the experience of love that a human being can know himself, can love what he is and will become, and find the fullness of life that is the glory of God. Only in love can man find cause for perennial celebration.

CHAPTER THREE

It was the day my father died. It was a bleak, cold, and blustery day in January. In the small hospital room, I was supporting him in my arms, when his eyes suddenly widened with a look of awe I had never seen before. I was certain that the angel of death had entered the room. Then my father slumped back, and I lowered his head gently onto the pillow. I closed his eyes, and told my mother who was seated by the bedside praying:

"It's all over, Mom. Dad is dead."

She startled me. I will never know why these were her first words to me after his death. My mother said:

"Oh, he was so proud of you. He loved you so much."

Somehow I knew from my own reaction that these words were saying something very important to me. They were like a sudden shaft of light, like a startling thought I had never before absorbed. Yet there was a definite edge of pain, as though I were going to know my father better in death than I had ever known him in life.

Later, while a doctor was verifying death, I was leaning against the wall in the far corner of the room, crying softly. A nurse came over to me and put a comforting arm around me. I couldn't talk through my tears. I wanted to tell her:

"I'm not crying because my father is dead. I'm crying because my father never told me that he was proud of me. He never told me that he loved me. Of course, I was expected to know these things. I was expected to know the great part I played in his life and the great part I occupied of his heart, but he never told me."

68

love and communication

love works for those who work at it

No matter how romanticists have tried to color it ever-sweet, and despite the sardonic claim of cynics that it is overrated, love is the tough, essential answer to the riddle of human existence, of human wholeness and happiness. To live is to love. Still it must be conceded that the cynics have a good set of statistics. It's not just the backlog of business in the divorce courts. It's the general fragmentation of the human family, parents against children, brothers against brothers, etc. If love really is the answer, it seems quite certain that the efforts of humans to find this answer in love-relationships have a high mortality rate. Love works if people will work at it. But why does love so often fail? What is the "work" which love demands, and why are we sometimes unwilling to undertake it?

the "work" of love

Love supposes, is, and does many things, but basically it is practiced in the act of *sharing*. To the extent and depth that two people are committed to each other in a love-relationship, to that extent and on that level they must actively share each other's life. Another word for sharing is *communication,* the act by which people share something or have it in common. If I communicate a secret of mine to you, we then share it, have it in common. To the extent that I communicate myself as a person to you and you communicate yourself to me, we share in common the mysteries of ourselves. Conversely, to the extent that we withdraw from each other and refuse mutual transparency, love is diminished.

In this context, communication not only is the life-blood of love and the guarantee of its growth, but is the very essence of love in practice. Love is sharing and sharing is communication. So when we say that communication is the "secret of staying in love" what we are really saying is that the secret of staying in love is to love, to keep sharing, to keep living out one's commitment. Of course, there is a first "yes," a first commitment made to love, but this first "yes" has an endless number of smaller "yeses" inside it.

One of the most common escapes from the practice of realities like love is the substitution of discussion for doing. We would rather debate, think about, and question these realities than put them into practice. It is much easier to discuss truths than to live them. Today, for example, there is much discussion about Christianity as a way of life: Can we still believe? What do we really believe? Is faith essential to happiness? The most obvious failing in the whole history of Christianity is that we have wandered into abstract and endless discussions instead of putting faith into practice. Uncommitted onlookers have been begging us not to entertain them with a debate about our doubts. They are asking: Show me what it would be like if I did believe and commit myself.

It is the same way with love. We would rather discuss it than live it. There is no price of admission to the forums of discussion, but the practice of love is a costly discipleship. Dag Hammarskjöld writes in his book *Markings:*

The "great" commitment all too easily obscures the "little" one. But without the humility and warmth which you have to develop in your relations to the few with whom you are personally involved, you will never be able to do anything for the many. Without them, you will live in a world of abstractions, where . . . your greed for power, and your death-wish lack the one opponent which is stronger than they—love. . . . It is better for the health of the soul to make one man good than "to sacrifice oneself for mankind."

unity not happiness

In rendering to love its required "work" or effort, it is important that we seek unity, not happiness. Those who set out upon the journey of love must strive for that transparency, that sharing and community of life which is the heart of love. Would-be lovers must not be constantly taking their temperatures and counting their pulsebeats to keep an up-to-the-minute check on how well they feel or how happy they are. A sense of well-being and happiness, as Viktor Frankl so often warns us, can come into a human life only as a by-product. You have no doubt heard this verse:

Happiness is like a butterfly.
The more you chase it, the more it will elude you.
But if you turn your attention to other things,
It comes and softly sits on your shoulder.

To be truly happy in love, a person must want unity, oneness, sharing. Sometimes this unity involves many things that are painful: honesty when you would rather lie a little, talking-out when you would rather pout, admitting embarrassing feelings when you would rather blame someone, standing there when you would rather run, admitting doubt when you would rather pretend certainty, and confronting when you would rather settle for peace at any price. None of these things, which are among the just demands of love, brings immediate peace and happiness; they bring immediate pain and struggle. Yes, love works if we will work at it. The work of love is to achieve a total honesty and transparency, and these are very difficult attainments. So people who run in a direct chase after the butterfly of happiness in love relationships will be empty-handed and empty-hearted in the end. Unity not happiness is the stern condition of success at love.

dialogue vs discussion

I would like to introduce here a distinction, based on content, between two types of communication. The first is the communication or sharing of emotions or feelings, which I would like to call *dialogue*. The second type of communication is the sharing of thoughts, values, the making of plans or decisions together, and, in general, things of a predominantly intellectual nature. This I would like to call *discussion*. Of course, this is an arbitrary distinction, and I am sure that not everyone would want to make it or would accept my usage of the words. It really is not important if others like or want to use the distinction, as long as what I am trying to say is clear. I need this or some such distinction to make a point which I think is tremendously important.

My point is this: There must be an emotional clearance (dialogue) between two involved partners in a love-relationship before they can safely enter into a deliberation (discussion) about plans, choices, values. The assumption behind this distinction and the priority given to dialogue is that the breakdown in human love and communication is *always* due to *emotional* problems. Two people in love can continue to deepen in their affection for each other while holding opposite opinions in almost any area of life. These contrary intellectual persuasions do not become an obstacle to love until one or both of the parties feels emotionally threatened.

73

In the first chapter of this book, we said that the essential need of human nature is self-esteem, self-appreciation, and self-celebration. I can give up almost anything while holding myself and my world together, but I cannot forfeit self-esteem without profound repercussions in my whole life. Most of us have a whole gamut of emotions, especially expressions and emotions of hostility, ready to be detonated in case of threat to self-esteem. Anger in a love-relationship arises because we have somehow felt threatened and afraid. My feeling of worth, the joy of being me, and the inner cause I have for self-celebration have been endangered. It is as simple as that; it is as complicated as that. But the point here is that, while my emotions are throbbing with these fears, angers, and self-defensive urges, I am in no condition to have an open-minded, honest, and loving discussion with you or with anyone else. I will need the emotional clearance and ventilation of dialogue before I will be ready for this discussion.

The detour which must at all costs be avoided is to mistake an issue which belongs to discussion— e.g., how much you spent for that new coat or whether I fixed the broken door—for the real gut issue of personal security, which belongs in the realm of dialogue. Lovers, it has been said, rarely argue about the *real* issue.

We have said that love, unlike money, cannot be banked. There must be a continuous, mutual and reciprocal support of personal worth in a love-relationship. When there is prolonged deprivation of this reinforcement, the "bankrupt" feeling sets in, with the accompanying options to ease the pain of this feeling of fundamental failure. The problem is, of course, essentially *emotional:* how do I *feel* about myself, my worth, my life? Everything else is symptomatic. All other emotional turbulence, whatever form it takes, is only a ripple from this central agony.

More often than not we fail to realize that our problems are basically emotional, and that we suffer most from those emotions which arise when our sense of worth is threatened. The consequence of this lack of awareness is the so called "displaced emotion." The way I am treated at my place of work or at my school may cause me to doubt my own worth, with the resultant fear that no one could really esteem, love, or care about me. This is the kind of threat to selfhood that usually surfaces not as fear (which it really is) but as hostility, a self-defensive anger. When enough of this anger gathers in us, without the release and perspective afforded by dialogue, the setting is ripe for displacement of emotions. The kid leaves a roller skate in the driveway, the wife is late with dinner, or the sympathetic question of a well intentioned parent is interpreted as "being nosey"—and all hell breaks loose. We are, of course, perfectly sure that our hostility is righteous indignation, the kind Jesus felt when he threw the buyers and sellers out of the temple. Anyone would get angry, we are sure, under such circumstances. But the anger and frustration we feel is really displaced. At its roots, the problem is the same old one. We feel somehow diminished in self-respect and we are acting out our anger on the nearest available victim.

dialogue:
the gift of self

We have been saying that dialogue must precede discussion because the static of unresolved and unexpressed emotions will block all attempt at the open, free-flowing exchange that leads to plans, decisions, etc. The presumption has been that these emotions are negative, and obviously not all emotions are negative. In the case of positive emotions, there is an even more compelling motive to practice dialogue before discussion. I become a transparent, knowable individual to you only when I tell you my feelings. My ideas, convictions, values, persuasions are really not original with me. I have got them from reading, by inhaling traditions, by listening to and imitating others, by the inevitable osmosis of human contagion. My ideas and the stances I take can locate me in a category, like "Irish," "Catholic," or "Democrat," but they can never make me transparent and knowable, so that you can experience me, share my person. Only my feelings, positive-negative-neutral, do this. My feelings are like my fingerprints, the color of my eyes, and the sound of my voice: unique to me and unrepeatable in anyone else. To know me you must know my feelings. And only when you know *me* through dialogue, at any moment in my life, will you be able to understand my ideas, preferences, and intentions, shared in discussion.

If anyone thinks for a moment about this, he will realize the truth involved. Perhaps you know someone, a teacher, a neighbor, a local clergyman, anyone who trades in ideas, theories, teachings, techniques, etc., but who keeps his communications carefully sterilized and bloodless, strained completely of all emotional content. I once listened to such a man for eight days, in a series of lectures, and I was sure at the end that I did not know him at all. I wasn't even sure whether he was parroting a book he had read, and I wondered how old his "notes" were and to how many people he had read them. I have noticed that when I myself am the public speaker, audiences "turn on" when I am willing to offer them my feelings, not as a demagogue seeking to manipulate, but quietly as a brother wanting

There must be an
emotional clearance
between the two partners.

to share. I have watched this truth proved again and again in public forums, in classrooms, in living room conversation, and in one-to-one communication. My emotions are the key to me. When I give you this key, you can come into me, and share with me the most precious gift I have to offer you: myself.

Important Footnote: The emphasis in this section on dialogue is on the communication of emotions. The central thesis is that when I tell you my emotions or feelings I am telling you who I really am, I am giving you myself. While all this is absolutely true, it might at the same time seem to be saying that you *are* your emotions. This is not true at all. You and I are much more than our emotions. We have fears, but we are more than fear. We get angry, but we are more than our angers. We have minds to know, to make decisions, accept and absorb values. We have wills, too, the heart to love and belong, to be committed and loyal. Please read, if you have time, what I have written in *Why Am I Afraid to Tell You Who I Am?* on the integration of the emotions by the mind and will. As essential as our emotions are to communication, they do *not* make our decisions for us. Only the perpetual child is ruled by his feelings.

Still, it is true and cannot be emphasized too much that only when I share my feelings in gut-level communication am I truly sharing myself. It is true that my values, beliefs, and goals are more important than my feelings, but only when I tell you how I feel about my values, beliefs, and goals will you be able to perceive my uniqueness. It is true that my love is more important than my feelings, but only when I share with you the many feelings that my love stirs in me will you be able to see my love as unique and unrepeatable. The diamond is the person, but the setting that brings out and illustrates all the facets of beauty is the feelings. Without the setting the diamond couldn't be seen and admired. Without the feelings, the person cannot be known.

the "peak" experience

At each point in our lives we represent a confluence of many things. At the center, of course, is the self-image, but feeding into this central fact of personhood, like spokes moving towards a hub, are many other currents and forces. These are the people and events in our lives which can be sources of great personal enrichment. However, in the defensive posture of a person who has had his ego dented and does not want to risk further vulnerability, most of us move into one security operation or another. We guardedly filter the reality that gets through to us from these currents and forces in our lives. And so life goes on for most of us, pretty much on a plateau. Each yesterday begins to look a lot like today and each today will resemble tomorrow. This is the setting for stagnation in which there is nothing left but to look for a few "kicks," or collect status symbols to be looked at as an old football hero looks at his trophies. This is the portrait of a person who is only 10% alive, who was made to travel on 8 cylinders but who is using only one.

It would be futile to confront him. Confrontation would very probably only scare him, and he would have to react angrily, to launch out in some kind of a hostile offense, which is said to be the best defense. He would ask us: "Who the hell do you think you are, anyway?" Sensitivity sessions, so popular in the sixties, that have tried this brutal, frontal assault on human security operations have been reviewed as more dangerous than helpful. So called "teachable" moments are rarely if ever occasioned by ripping off masks, leaving people nakedly aware of their own failures. There is an enormous risk that they would only go deeper inside themselves.

We get out of the rut, above the plateau, out of a living death, only through "peak" experiences of communication. In a fuller perspective, occurrence or non-occurrence of these peak experiences is what makes or breaks a love-relationship. Without these moments of breakthrough into new and mutual transparency, love becomes dull, stagnant, and boring. Lovers start scratching around elsewhere, looking for some action, some ego-stimulation. In the garden of humanity what is not growing is dying.

Let me try now to describe what I mean by peak experience in communication, and then give you an example from my own life. First of all, I presume that in such a peak experience one of the persons opens himself in such a way that the other is called out of himself and out of all his old and fixed positions, out of his old calculations, into a new experience. This new experience is not only a deeper knowledge of the reality of his partner, but also by later refraction and assimilation it will be a new experience of his own capacity and reality. Such an experience will leave that reality forever changed, more open, more loving, more alive.

Since emotions are what define and reveal the essential me, I will necessarily be revealing my *feelings* in the moment of my transparency. It is the sharing of my feelings that will provide you with the

My feelings are like my fingerprints,
the color of my eyes,
and the sound of my voice:
unique to me and unrepeatable.

opportunity to know me in a new way, to know yourself in a new way, and to be changed by that knowledge. Perhaps it will be in the context of relating an incident or expressing my love, but it will be the feeling or emotional content that will carry the charge and offer the experience of my person. Unless I open my feelings, you will simply "project" into me your own emotions. For example, if I tell you that I have failed in some way without describing vividly my exact emotional reaction to the failure, you will anticipate that my reaction was what yours would be in a similar situation; and it never, never is. You will, if I deny you my emotional depths, never get to know me, or be enriched by the kind of peak experience being described here.

Why do these peak experiences have such a profound effect? First of all, it is obvious that people are transformed by their relationships with those who are closest to them. Peak experiences of communication inject a new vitality into these relationships. When you open to me a part of yourself, a reaction, a hurt, a tenderness or a fear that I have never before experienced in you, I am made more aware of your depth and your mystery. I no longer take you for granted, or foolishly believe that I know you so completely that I need not look for anything new, as though you will always be the unchangeable you that I first met and loved.

Secondly, these peak moments help me to get out of myself. While I am inside myself there is no possibility of change. This is just as certain as the old saying that we cannot learn anything new while we are speaking but only when listening. Imprisonment in self is a small, lonely, and incredibly dull world with its population of one. There is no real interaction and so there is no growth or change. When you open the depths of your feelings and yourself to me, it invites me to break my preoccupation with myself. It calls me out of the boring sameness that preoccupation with self produces. When this happens, when I go out of myself, the door locks behind me. I can never go back into that small, rigid, fixed little world again. Perhaps such dramatization makes peak experience sound too apocalyptic and the resulting change unrealistically sudden and deep. Change is always slow, but the fact of change and the hope of transformation are very real.

The experience of peak communication has been compared to a person who stays in his apartment alone all day. While there he has a feeling of safety. There is no necessity to interact with other people who may threaten or actually hurt him. He knows where everything is, the night lamp, the bathroom, the Pepto Bismol. He is at least secure from harm in his stagnation. The whole world outside his little apartment is lost on him. He is alive but not very. He is breathing but not really living. Then one day he looks out his window and sees another person who is experiencing a moment of emotional intensity. It is so interesting, so captivating that he forgets about all his fears. He unlocks the door, he goes out to the other and for that lovely, liberating moment he experiences another world. He breathes a new and fresh air. The light and warmth of the sun fall on him for the first time. And then he knows something. The life in him has been expanded. He can never go back, never be the same again, or live the same narrow, cramped existence. He wouldn't fit in that world anymore, and all because he has been drawn out of himself to someone else in a profound way. All the dimensions of his world, the anticipations and prejudices in which he has been imprisoned to some extent fall away.

In the wake of peak experiences, both partners are permanently, even if not always dramatically, altered because the whole relationship acquires a new depth and intensity. There will be a new perspective in which each will see the other.

Let me now share with you one such experience from my own life. About five years ago, the doctors told our family that my aged mother very probably had an inoperable cancer of the liver, which had to be considered terminal. To confirm the tentative diagnosis of their tests, the doctors wished to perform exploratory surgery, to which we all agreed. On the night before the surgery, I carefully informed my mother of her condition, so that she could face the mystery of death in a fully human way. I sat nervously on the edge of her hospital bed, and asked if she would like to "go to confession." In the Catholic church, the members of a priest's family usually go to another priest for the Sacrament of Penance, or "confession" as it is popularly called. However, because my mother suffered from a severe arthritis in the latter years of her life, I became her "Confessor" of choice for the ten years preceding the time of the episode which I am now relating.

I must also tell you that I am the youngest of my mother's three children, her "baby." I swear that I can sense this word in her voice when she speaks to me and in her face whenever she looks at me. There is one exception: while she is making one of her angelic "confessions." At this moment I become her "priest," her "Father." At these moments she seems totally transformed by her faith in me as God's representative. All the sounds and sights of "baby" disappear.

On the night before the surgery, I heard what I thought might well be her last confession, and as usual it was so saintly that for me it was an exercise

We get out of the rut
only through "peak" experiences
of communication.

in humility. At the conclusion, I assured her that I was bringing to God her sorrow and to her God's forgiveness. To the extent of my ability to be in touch with God and with her, I felt that I must also bring her God's message, the things I thought God would say to her at this face-to-face-with-death moment. The heart of the message I bore was this: "Thank you. Thanks for all the nights you sat up with sick children, for all the silent prayers you said for them, for all the cups of cool water you patiently poured, for all the clothes you sewed and mended, for all the sandwiches you made and wrapped in wax paper, for all the times. . . . " She listened attentively and almost dutifully because I was her "Father."

After the absolution and final blessing of the sacramental rite, I instantly became her child again, and she tenderly cupped my bent head in her hands, and cradled it in a motherly way on her shoulder. She then turned her lips to my ear: "John," she said, "don't be sad now. Don't be sad for me. If it isn't tomorrow morning, it will be some other morning, and if it isn't this year, it will be some other year. Besides, Daddy's been waiting a long time for me. I am all ready now to go meet him. And you—you have been called to a beautiful life, to do beautiful things for God and for the people you serve. If you feel sad for me, it will take your mind and heart away from your life and your work. Don't let that happen. Don't be sad for me. Remember, if it isn't tomorrow morning, it will be another morning, and if it isn't this year, it will be another. Don't be sad now." Then she kissed me.

It was like the moment after my father's death. I was crying softly again and couldn't talk, but this time the reason for my tears was different. I had known my mother in this moment more profoundly than ever before, in a moment when she was

86

courageously rising to the occasion of dying, a moment when people are usually reduced to what they really are, no more, no less.

As it turned out, it was not her life that God was asking. The next morning the surgeon came from the operation smiling, assuring us that the suspected cancer was not found, and that the condition causing mother to feel ill was corrected. He said we could see her briefly in the intensive care unit of the hospital. There we found her conscious but cranky. My sister tried to brush back the hairs which had been matted on her forehead, and she complained that the brush was pulling her hair. She even complained that there was no TV in intensive care. Nothing, not even the good news that she was on the road to recovery, seemed to please her. I stood off at a distance, smiling. "Go ahead, Old Girl," my heart was saying, "let it all out. Your mind is foggy and your body hurts. And that's the way it is in the dust and struggle of daily life. But there is one big difference now. Last night I got to know you. Beneath the words that come out of your mouth without passing through your mind or heart, beneath all the temporary, turbulent, superficial complaints you never really meant, I knew you. And I will always know something about you that will make all of these other moments seem much less important. And some day, when you really have gone to be with God and with Dad, most of all I will remember what you said to me last night, what you meant to me last night."

As the song says, "It only takes a moment to be loved a whole life through." I don't know if this is literally true but I do believe that the depth and duration of a love-relationship will depend on those occasional moments of meeting called "peak experiences."

in settings
of struggle

The story of my mother is a sweet story with a sweet ending. It could easily mislead one to believe that dialogue is always easy and inevitably leads to peak moments, after which people live happily ever after. It is not so, of course. We must never construe dialogue as a pain killing aspirin or peak experiences as a kind of raw liquor that results in a permanent "high." Laying yourself on the line in the self-disclosure of dialogue will challenge all the courage, determination, and faith that you can muster. The most universal fear of all men is to be found out, to be known and then to be rejected. In fact, I suspect that many people do not hear the vocation to dialogue or refuse to be converted to its gospel of "unity not happiness" because of this fear. We all know that it is risky. Misunderstanding and rejection really hit where it hurts. But more profoundly, if I admitted to myself the deepest feelings that stir in me, it is possible that I might lose the self-respect and self-appreciation that I need so desperately. It is much easier to *discuss a problem* because I can always change my mind. It is much harder to *expose a feeling* because somehow instinctively I know that I am exposing the place where I really live. It is much easier to give you a box of candy or a box of cigars than to give you myself in self-disclosure. There is very little risk in giving you candy but when I give you myself I am putting myself at the mercy of your understanding and acceptance. It is much easier to be busy, very busy, doing a million things for you than to sit down with you trustfully and tell you who I really am, how I really feel about you, about myself, about us, about our past, present and future. But the fact of the matter is that I give you

Sharing
my feelings
will provide you with
the opportunity to know me
in a new way,
to know yourself in a new way,
and be changed.

nothing until I give you this gift. There is no other secret of staying in love or growing in love.

one picture
worth a thousand words

If only I could make a movie of the following true story, it would illustrate better than many words what I am trying to say. A young couple had reached the brink of divorce. The husband, in general a very good and well-intentioned man, had a "weakness" which had bothered him since adolescence, but which he had kept carefully concealed from his wife and everyone else . . . till the night he was arrested for his "weakness" and the lid came off.

For several days following the embarrassment of arrest, the young wife and mother reflected on her situation and on the possibility of the future. She decided that she was not equal to this struggle and wanted a divorce. She said that she could not live with the uncertainty of possible future embarrassments. However, she was asked by a counselor to postpone her divorce action on the grounds that her husband's recovery depended more on her loving acceptance of him than on any other human factor or form of therapy. She agreed to try. However, during the next three months there were several recurrences of the problem, although no arrests. In this period her decision became definite: she wanted a divorce.

When they entered the office of the marriage counselor, they were walking at a distance of four or five feet, their eyes carefully avoiding each other. Anger rasped at the edge of their voices.

"I must have a divorce. I can't go on like this!"

"And if she wants a divorce, she can have it. I'm sick and tired of this whole mess, of her hounding. She's always accusing...."

It was a clear case of attempted discussion without previous dialogue. The counselor calmly seated the two angry, threatened, and threatening people, and asked for an emotional clearance, requesting that there be no judgments, no accusations, no resurrection of past history. He insisted on straight dialogue: *just feelings.*

The wife began by announcing that her "central" feeling was insecurity. She said she thought that she knew her husband till she found out about this strange weakness which he had hidden from her. She felt that this weakness owned some part of him that was not hers and made her jealous. She had personified his weakness and saw it as her competitor. She thought she could have coped with the challenge of another woman, but not this. She was encouraged to continue describing this feeling of insecurity until it became very vivid to all. Both the husband and counselor could feel the texture, taste the loneliness and hear the agony of her insecurity. Then, by invitation, she continued to describe in a similarly graphic way the other emotions which she was feeling at this time in the context of the problem. She described her sadness, her loneliness, her disappointment in herself and her own lack of strength to cope with the situation. She described an almost constant bewilderment and fear for the future. She felt that the divorce action was an escape. She personally felt like a small child running away from something she couldn't face.

Judging from his reactions, the husband had heard none of this before. The anger with which he had previously regarded his wife turned into a puzzled, wide-eyed wonder and even hope. After a half hour of excellent description of her feelings, the wife was asked by the counselor if she didn't feel some anger, some desire for vengeance, some desire to hurt her husband in retaliation for the anguish he had caused her. Tears welled up in her eyes, and she admitted that each time the thought of vengeance or retaliation occurred to her, it was immediately drowned in feelings of deep compassion and sorrow, not to mention affection. "I could never deliberately hurt you," she blurted out, "because I love you too much." The eyes of the husband, his ears and mind strained to embrace what he was hearing and seeing.

Then, in his time, he described his feelings, his central emotion of shame, a feeling of alienation, separation from others. "I have heard and read that others are troubled with my problem, but I am the only one I know of. I feel like I am different and separated from the rest of the human race. I feel like a leper turned away by society." He graphically described his fear of psychologically infecting his children with his problem, of projecting into them an inclination to the weakness that had made his own life a private hell. He told of putting them out of his lap when this thought and feeling came to terrorize him.

In the most sensitive part of his emotional admission, she put a tremulous hand on his knee in a kind of non-verbal way of saying: "I am with you. I will stay with you." Almost as though the floodgates had been opened and there was a feeling of release, the husband went on and on through a whole gamut of emotions: shame, fear, loneliness, alienation, despair. Finally, this man of large muscular stature admitted a strong emotional desire to be held in someone's arms, in the arms of someone with whom he wouldn't be ashamed to cry like the little boy who was somewhere inside him.

At this point, both people arose, embraced, and cried together. When the tears were exhausted, they were smiling at each other, looking at each other appreciatively and compassionately. One hour before this they were determined to leave each other forever. After this hour of dialogue, they looked at and held each other as though nothing could ever separate them. They were two good and decent people who almost didn't get to know each other.

This story, too, has a happy ending. But no doubt these people will have many other problems, and perhaps there will even be moments in the future when the bond of their love will again be threatened, but if they have learned the necessity of dialogue as the lifeblood of love they will be all right. The tinsel will turn into gold.

The partners in a love-relationship must realize that breakdown in communication is emotional in origin. They must learn to share their feelings, to dialogue before attempting discussion. They must be willing to risk transparency in the quest for that unity of knowledge and acceptance from which alone happiness can result as a by-product. They must be willing to work towards those occasional moments of "peak experience" which vitalize, deepen, and transform a love relationship. With and in such willingness they have learned a valuable secret: the secret of staying and growing in love.

CHAPTER FOUR

The Marriage Enrichment week-end was over. There was the usual amount of incense in the air, and I enjoyed it. I returned to Chicago with a warm, complacent feeling about all those couples initiated into the art of dialogue, getting to know each other, learning to love each other more deeply. Someone had said to me as I was leaving: "Thanks for giving us to each other." I cherished the compliment all the way back to Chicago, savoring it like an all-day sucker because it expressed my deepest ambition and most sincere intention. Then, after a week, came the following letter:

"You and your dammed dialogue! I have just found out that my husband has felt lonely all during the ten years of our marriage. I thought we had a happy marriage. Now I feel like a failure, and he's still lonely. So you open your guts. Then what? You started this. What are you going to do for us now?"

I sat with the letter for a long time, pondering what I would answer.

about those emotions

no one can cause emotions in another

In learning to understand ourselves we must learn to become very open to and accepting of all our emotional reactions. If what we have said about our emotions is the key to personal understanding, then we must learn to listen to our own emotions if we are to become growing persons. The basic belief in

95

which I must repose absolute faith in order to understand myself by understanding my emotions is this: no one else can cause or be responsible for my emotions. Of course, we feel better assigning our emotions to other people. "You made me angry... You frightened me... You made me jealous," etc. The fact is that you can't make me anything. You can only *stimulate* the emotions that are already in me, waiting to be activated. The distinction between *causing* and *stimulating* emotions is not just a play on words. The acceptance of the truth involved is critical. If I think you can make me angry, then when I become angry I simply lay the blame and pin the problem on you. I can then walk away from our encounter learning nothing, concluding only that you were at fault because you made me angry. Then I need to ask no questions of myself because I have laid all the responsibility at your feet.

If I accept the thesis that others can only *stimulate* emotions already latently present in me, when these emotions do surface it becomes a learning experience. I then ask myself: Why was I so afraid? Why did that remark threaten me? Why was I so angry? Was my anger really a disguised way of saving face? Something was already in me that this incident called forth. What was it? A person who really believes this will begin dealing with his emotions in a profitable way. He will no longer allow himself the easy escape into the judgment and condemnation of others. He will become a growing person, more and more in touch with himself.

in every emotion
a self-revelation

I remember receiving a very bitter letter several years ago. The author of the letter accused me of being a "sadist...a bully...a megalomaniac...." My reaction was very mild and sympathetic. I knew the writer of the letter must have deep problems, and I wondered how I could help him. The letter stirred in me only compassion. I felt no negative emotions because I did not believe the accusations. I know that I am not a sadist or a bully. I am not even a megalomaniac. The incident helped me to discover in myself a deep and warm compassion.

Several weeks later I was happily bantering with two of my students, and in the playful interchange one of them remarked: "Do you know that you come across to some people as a phoney?" Suddenly playtime was over. I pompously demanded a definition of "phoney." The two embarrassed students tried to back away, insisting that they themselves didn't think of me as a phoney, but it was not enough. A gush of white-hot anger had arisen in me, and I pressed on for a definition. Finally one of the students said: "I guess being a phoney means that you don't practice what you preach."

Having anticipated such a definition, I immediately pleaded guilty. I knew that I was on safe ground, being able to point out that no one really lives up to his own ideals or translates his intentions perfectly into action. Then I pointed out a second meaning of phoney, namely that one does not practice what he preaches because he does not even believe what he preaches. To this charge, I solemnly pleaded innocent. The bloodletting completed with surgical precision, I dismissed my victims. Of course, I realized immediately that I had been very angry and that I had been very unfair because of my anger.

This is the critical moment. The only real mistake is the one from which we learn nothing. In the aftermath of an encounter such as I have just described, there are two options. One can go off in a huff, ranting about stupid and ungrateful kids, or he can look into himself to find the reason for his own emotions. This is the essential difference between a growing and non-growing person, between authenticity and self-deception. On this one occasion, at least, I chose to be growing and authentic. I looked within myself, and listened carefully to the anger which was gradually subsiding, and I found that it grew out of a deep-seated fear in me that maybe I am a phoney, even in the second sense. I could react mildly in the face of an accusation that I am a sadist, a bully, or a megalomaniac, but the accusation of being a phoney touches an exposed nerve-ending in me. Sometimes I am afraid that I talk a better game than I am able to live, with the subsequent fear that maybe I don't fully believe all that I preach. (P.S. I did apologize to the students. I admitted to them the source of my anger and explained what I had found out about myself.)

We are saying that there is something already in us that explains our emotional reactions, but this does not mean that what is in us is bad or regrettable. The fear I have that there is a discrepancy between the word level and the commitment of my life is not bad or regrettable. It is me. Likewise, I may become angry at seeing a bully picking on a defenseless victim, and find that the source of my anger, the thing which is inside me, is a healthy sense of justice and an active compassion for the underdogs of this world.

The important thing is the realization that every emotional reaction is telling us something about ourselves. We must learn not to assign these reactions to others, preferring to blame them rather than to learn something about ourselves. When I do react emotionally, I know that not everyone would react as I have. Everyone does not have the same stored-up emotions which I have. In dealing simultaneously with many people, there is a great variety of emotional reactions. They are different people, have different needs; they come out of a different past and are seeking different goals. Consequently, their emotional reactions are different because of something inside each of them. The most I ever do is to stimulate these emotions. Similarly, if I want to know something about myself, my needs, my self-image, my sensitivity, my psychological programing and my values, then I must listen very sensitively to my own emotions.

human emotions: the iceberg principle

It is estimated that a floating iceberg is only one-tenth visible. Nine-tenths of the ice block remains submerged beneath the surface of the water. A similar estimate has been suggested with regard to human emotions. The part that we are able to see is only about one-tenth of the total reality. The implication of this suggestion is not that people show only one-tenth of their true, recognized feelings to others, but rather that they are themselves consciously aware of only a small part of their own emotions. We hide the bulk of our emotions even from ourselves by the subconscious defense mechanism called repression.

Of course, non-expression of emotions is very common. Many human emotions, inwardly recognized, are never expressed. For example, "I'll never let her know that I am jealous." There are two basic reasons for this non-expression of recognized feelings: first, we may doubt that others would understand. They would certainly wonder about us, and possibly would question either our sanity or our integrity. Such doubt invades that sensitive area in us, the center of human behavior and existence: our self-image and consequent self-acceptance-appreciation-celebration. The second possible motive for non-expression of emotions is even more frightening. I fear that my emotional admissions could be used against me, either thoughtlessly or cruelly. You might bring it up later, and even if you don't bring it up explicitly, I will always wonder if you are pitying me, afraid of me, or distancing yourself from me because of the feelings I have confided to you.

Non-expression is not good, but the repression of emotions into the subconscious is even more self-destructive because, while we know that we are hurting when we have repressed our true feelings, we do not know why. We have hidden the source of pain in the "dungeon" of the subconscious. Repressed emotions unfortunately do not die. They refuse to be silenced. They pervasively influence the whole personality and behavior of the repressor. For example, a person who represses guilt feelings is forever, though subconsiously, trying to punish

The only real mistake
is the one from which
we learn nothing.

himself. He will never allow himself success or enjoyment without qualification. Repressed fears and angers may be "acted out" physically as insomnia, headaches, or ulcers. If such fears and angers had been consciously accepted and reported in detail to another, there would have been no necessity for the sleeplessness, the tension headaches or ulcers.

the reasons for our repression

There are three general motives for this emotional repression. We bury undesirable emotions because: 1) *We have been programed to do this.* The so-called "parent-tapes" of our early indoctrination are constantly replaying their messages in us. Our deepest instincts have been educated in the first five years of our lives by our parents and others who have influenced us. A child from a non-demonstrative family will certainly have a tendency to repress emotions of tenderness and affection. A child who grows up in a constantly fighting family may be very comfortable with the acknowledgement and expression of anger, but trained to repress the gentler emotions of compassion, remorse, etc.

2) *We "moralize" emotions.* Depending on our background, we tend to label certain emotions "good" or "bad." For example, it is good to feel grateful but bad to feel angry or jealous. Foolishly but factually parents often tell their children: "You have *no right* to feel that way," or "You *shouldn't* feel angry; you *ought* to feel sorry for him." For some reason, the one valid emotion that our society has

almost universally quarantined out of sight is feeling sorry for oneself, the emotion of self-pity. Indeed, self-pity has become a dirty word.

3) The final consideration that prompts us to deny certain valid human feelings is a *"value conflict."* For example, if "being a man" has become an important part of my identity and self-image, a value upon which I place high premium, certain emotions will almost certainly be considered damaging to this image. I will have to edit my emotions carefully to preserve my masculinity. For the first forty years of my life, I personally could not admit fear of anyone or anything. At least that is what my head kept thinking and my mouth kept saying. But my poor stomach bore the brunt of my repression. Somehow my intestines did not really believe my head and my mouth. I preferred Gelusil to the truth.

I am not sure that all three of these motives cannot be reduced to one simple motive. What I need in order to go on living is self-acceptance-esteem-appreciation-celebration. I have tried to build up some kind of structure that will allow me this needed self-acceptance. I admit that it is like a house of match sticks. I must protect it from all threats: those that come from within as well as those which come from the outside. Emotions arising from within, if they are judged incompatible with self-acceptance, might endanger the precarious, leaning tower of my self-image. I cannot have that. So I have headaches, allergies, ulcers, virus colds and spastic parts. Buried emotions are like rejected people; they make us pay a high price for having rejected them. Hell hath no fury like that of a scorned emotion.

the real loss
of lost emotions

Lost or repressed emotions are not really lost. They continue, in one way or another, to remind us that we really didn't get away with the attempted rejection. Aside from this built-in system of painful sanctions, the essential tragedy of repression is that the whole process of human growth is shut down, at least temporarily. Psychologists call this state "fixation," an arrest of growth and development.

I think that this truth about living has been very dramatically illustrated in the research and writing on death and dying by Dr. Elisabeth Kübler-Ross. What the Doctor writes about acceptance of death seems to apply equally well to the acceptance of self and the realities of life. Both acts of acceptance require a process of emotional reactions, each of which must be fully experienced for the successful completion of the process.

Dr. Ross theorizes that the terminal patient, after being informed of approaching death, rarely if ever is capable of immediate and full acceptance. He must pass through various stages, the first of which is a stage of *denial:* "No, not me." Unable to cope with the fact that life for him will soon be over, he erases the handwriting on the wall by denial. When he drops his denial, he usually, according to the research of Ross, enters into a period of *anger, rage and indignation.* His "Not me" becomes "Why me?" He is raging against the dying of the light and his anger is often by displacement directed to hospital personnel. He is not really saying, "This food is cold . . . that injection hurt." He is really saying: "You are going to live. I am going to die. You are

Every emotional reaction
is telling us something
about ourselves.

going to raise your children and see your grand-children. I am going to be taken from my children before they are raised." He resents the hospital staff, not for any of the pretended reasons, but because they are healthy and have promise of continued life.

In the third stage, this edge of anger and rage mellows into a stance of *bargaining*. The "Why me?" becomes "Yes me, but maybe. . . ." The bargaining overtures are made to the doctor—"I'll never smoke again!" Or even to God—"I'll go to church every Sunday!"

The fourth stage is one of *resignation in depression:* "Yes me, damn it! I am going to die, and I am resigned to the inevitable fact, but I don't want to die." Externally, the patient goes through a period of silent reluctance and sadness, but he is at this stage confronting the fact of death more realistically. Of course, the final stage in the process is one of *acceptance*. "I am going to die. My life's work is over. I am ready." This final stage of acceptance is characterized externally in a quiet, silent peace.

The significant and relevant thing is what Dr. Ross says about the *process* of these stages. Like steps of a ladder, each one must be negotiated separately and usually in order. Ross warns that if anyone interferes with the process, trying to keep the patient in one stage, like denial, or move him from one to another before he is ready, the whole process moving towards acceptance is automatically shut down. Often families want a person who is dying to play the "denial game." Ninety-five per cent of all such patients are not really fooled, but the family will not let them go on into the more difficult emotions partly because they want to spare the dying person but also because they don't know how to handle and live with these more difficult emotions. Often we tell people not to cry in order to spare ourselves the necessity of having to cope with tears.

Dr. Ross relates that often a well-intentioned chaplain can attempt to move a person from emotions of resistance, like anger and indignation, into the theologically compatible emotion of acceptance. He waves over the head of the dying person the magic wand: "It is God's will." If the dying person tries to alter his emotional patterns to accommodate the chaplain, the process is over. The anger and indignation must be acknowledged and expended before acceptance becomes a possibility.

Dr. Ross tells of her own dealing with a dying woman who asked if there was a "screaming room" in the hospital. When Dr. Ross told her that there was a chapel where she could pray, the woman angrily replied: "If I felt like praying I would have asked for the chapel. I want to scream!"

The point of reviewing Dr. Ross' research is to suggest that there are not only essential, emotional stages on the way to the acceptance of death, but also a comparable process of stages on the way to the acceptance of self and life. Like the dying, those who would live fully must go through periods of denial, simply refusing to accept themselves as they are, by denying the facts of their own unique human condition. There are also periods of anger and bargaining, and a sad resignation. But if those who love them will stand by, holding out their own acceptance, without any attempt at emotional manipulation, the process will probably have a happy conclusion. The penalty for intrusion and emotional coercion in this self-acceptance process is the same as in the death-acceptance process: fixation.

The whole process will shut down. Like dust swept under a rug, the rejected emotions will be driven into the labyrinths of the subconscious, but the price will be extremely high. We must learn to welcome in ourselves and in others the fact of this emotional process and whatever feelings are a part of it. Each emotion is saying something, leading us somewhere.

The real loss of lost emotions is the loss of growth and ultimately the loss of that which is the central need of every human being: realistic self-acceptance, esteem, appreciation, and celebration.

locating lost emotions

Recovering our lost emotions is absolutely essential to human growth. To the extent that we repress, we lose contact with ourselves. We get lost behind our masks and security operations.

At the risk of oversimplification, I would like to suggest that, if you really want to listen to your emotions, they will speak to you. Whenever you are ready to stop telling your emotions what they should be, they will tell you what they really are. The discoverer of the subconscious, Sigmund Freud, says that all repressed emotions are constantly trying to break back into consciousness. As a result, according to Dr. Freud, we have to practice "reaction formation," or some other means of continued repression. We have to keep acting in a manner opposed to the emotions that are being repressed. For example, we assume a brave set of external mannerisms to compensate for the fear we are repressing. Since repressed emotions are trying to surface, they can be kept repressed only with some effort of this kind.

So the first thing we should do is to sit quietly and take a mental, emotional inventory. Do you really want to know what's buried in you? If a doctor offered to give you truth serum and record all your answers to his searching questions, would you be eager or reluctant to volunteer? Would you be ready to revise the suppositions that you have made about yourself? Would you be ready to admit that some of your alleged motives for action are really phoney? Could you face the fact that you are perhaps displacing emotions on innocent bystanders, blaming others for things you cannot accept in yourself? These are all possibilities, and they must be considered. How much do you love the truth and really want to know yourself?

My own answer is that I do want the full prescription but in small doses. I want the full story, but I think I can take only one chapter at a time. I don't feel strong enough because I don't love myself enough to face everything at once. I think that this is why so many people have been pushed over the brink into insanity by mind-expanding drugs. As one young experimenter said after his bad trip: "I've been to places inside myself where no one should ever go."

Fortunately nature is more kind and merciful than narcotics. The subconscious divulges its contents gradually in proportion to our strength. To the extent that we love, esteem, appreciate and celebrate our reality we are more flexible with the contents of the subconscious and more open to this whole process. To the extent that we are aware of our possession of many desirable qualities we will have the confidence to face what may be undesirable. So a willingness and even eagerness to know the truth is the point of departure. Only the full acceptance of the full truth can lead us to the fullness of life. Now for more specific methods.

free association in friendship

Psychoanalysis is the process of dredging the subconscious of its repressed contents and conflicts. In analysis the "fundamental rule" is called free association. The patient is directed not to prepare a report for the analyst, but to report spontaneously anything and everything that comes to mind, even though it may seem illogical or irrelevant. The patient tries to become as free as possible from external stimuli and conscious control. He is encouraged to verbalize whatever comes to mind, whatever feelings arise and whatever he suddenly remembers. The supposition is that all the burdens of the subconscious want release, and in the atmosphere of free association the patient is saying "yes," giving free rein to all his repressed impulses, emotions, ideas and experiences, which have been subconsciously reflected in his crippling attitudes and behavior.

There are many excellent analysts ready to help us with the process, which is long and expensive. Somehow I believe that this very process also can be achieved in true friendship, though I think that relatively few "friendships" accomplish the kind of freeing, spontaneous and reassuring atmosphere necessary for the release of these subconscious burdens. But the best advice is still, and will always be, to find a good friend and confidant. Find a person who accepts you in your ups and downs, and who will not hold you responsible to the logistical rules of coherence in your communication. And, if your friend becomes more manipulative than liberative, speak up. Convince him that his greatest contribution and assistance will be to help you find and face the truth about yourself.

psychosomatic self-analysis

There is another popular method of locating lost emotions, a technique evolved by Dr. Eugene T. Gendlin. Like all other theraputic techniques, it requires practice. I have found this to be of great help to myself on many occasions. The supposition of this theory is that people begin to make progress, sick people get better and healthy people become healthier, when they get in touch with their emotions and the reasons for those emotions. This, I think, is an almost universal supposition of modern psychology. Gendlin's theory also supposes that all repressed emotions somehow are "acted out" in physical symptoms, the most common of which are tension, fatigue, headaches, and respiratory or intestinal discomfort. In the technique suggested, one begins with a conscious awareness of his physical reactions, which are really repressed emotions translated into physical symptoms.

By an interior dialogue with his body, he welcomes the reconversion of the physical reaction into the original emotion. To verbalize this interior act, the person would say something like this to his headache: "You were an emotion, but I didn't want to experience you, so you have become a headache. Now I want you to come back. I will have you. I will be willing to feel whatever emotion you are." Under such invitation, the physical reaction is slowly changed back into a feeling—a feeling of fear, anger, etc. It may be accompanied by a fantasy like sinking in quicksand, or groping through a forest.

When the feeling has become relatively clear, the person then asks himself what might be the reasons for such a feeling. He will probably have to experiment with various hypotheses. But when he finally locates the true emotion and the full reason for it, the physical symptom will begin immediately to diminish and will disappear. The beauty of this system is that there is a built-in test of success: the disappearance of the physical reaction.

Perhaps an example from my own experience will help clarify this explanation. Several years ago I drove to Canada to make a preached-retreat of one week. The preacher had been highly recommended, and my first impressions were extremely favorable. Then anger began to build in me. I felt very irritable and noticed a growing aversion for both the retreat director and the other people in attendance. After four or five days, I was tense and troubled. I knew that I was repressing and displacing my emotions. What I saw, however, was only the tip of the iceberg. So I lay quietly on my bed, listened attentively to my own body with its tensions, the dull ache of my muscles, the slight pain in my neck and shoulders.

I invited these physical discomforts to reconvert into the emotions I had rejected. I invited those emotions to arise in me. If Freud is right that we must strain to keep repressed emotions repressed, relaxing in this way can be an important part of the process of recovering our lost emotions, but the essential thing is always the attitude of openness.

Out of somewhere deep inside me came not anger—my anger was like most anger, only a coverup—but a bleak and bitter sense of personal failure. It was clear after a matter of minutes that this was the true emotion I had repressed. This strange sense of failure became very strong in me. Then I began the final phase of this method of self-analysis, letting my mind range over various hypotheses. Could it be this...that? Then in a moment of sudden insight, it became very clear.

The retreat master was a saintly, loving and dedicated man. He appeared to be all the things that I wanted most to be but had not in fact become. Rather than accept my emotions of failure, stimulated by contact with such a holy man, I repressed them, and worked at the repression by a kind of reaction formation: feeling hostile towards the very man that I so deeply admired. At the moment I was willing to accept the feelings of my failure and acknowledge the reasons for those feelings, all tension drained out of me and, of course, there was no further need to displace my true feelings. I enjoyed a deep peace and most of all, I had learned something about myself, my deepest desire and my deepest pain.

the most popular method: transactional analysis

Transactional analysis originated with the late California psychiatrist, Eric Berne, as a method of "group" therapy. Berne believed that the starting point in therapy should be the transactions or interactions among the people in the group. Analysis of these transactions, he felt, would reveal the hidden or repressed emotional influences on behavior.

The man responsible for making T.A. available to the average person is a disciple of Berne, Dr. Thomas Harris, especially through his best-selling *I'm O.K.—You're O.K.* Harris proposes T.A. as a method of acknowledging repressed emotional factors in behavior, admitting that we are very profoundly influenced by others very early in life, but insisting that we are free and responsible for what we will become.

It is true that we are largely the product of past experience. Every event of our lives and the emotional reactions accompanying those events are recorded in our brains, in every muscle, cell and fiber of our being. So these events, and especially the feelings we associated with them, are always replaying inside of us, but most of this remains subconscious. We are rarely aware—without practice at T.A.—of the connection between our reaction to present events and this backlog of past experience and feeling. For example, I may have a hostile attitude or a fearful attitude towards all authority figures because my parents were domineering, but I may never be aware of this connection.

T.A. is a practical way of understanding these connections, of relating past emotional reactions, still lingering in us, to present experience and behavior. If a person is willing to act against inhibiting or crippling feelings, he will be able to change his habits of behavior, and consequently the course of his life. But the first necessity is to get to those buried feelings, and the starting point for this is to observe ourselves in action, in the transactions of every day.

Each of our interactions with another is a "transaction." In the normal transaction, one party offers a "stimulus," in word or gesture, and the other reacts with a transactional "response." The whole point of analyzing the transaction is to recognize and evaluate the underlying emotional influences of both the stimulus and the response.

Let us take an example. Transaction: Someone pays you a compliment. How do you react? Do you get wordy? Do you stammer? Do you change the topic? Do you blush or look away? Under your response lies an emotional backlog. What is this feeling under your reaction? Did you feel glad to be recognized? Were you happy but embarrassed to show it? The practice of T.A. promotes conscious awareness of such connection, so that we can effectively redirect our lives. Unless we see and act against crippling emotions our futures will be merely a playing out of previous programing. This is the most exciting feature of T.A. for most people: the hope that we can change. We can "move out of the tyranny of the past . . . to exercise self-direction and freedom of choice."

The theory of T.A. begins with the supposition of Alfred Adler that all human beings are afflicted with deep feelings of inferiority, a feeling of being "not O.K." Harris believes that most people never fulfill their human promise and potential because they remain perpetually helpless children overwhelmed by a sense of inferiority. The feeling of being O.K. does not imply that the person has risen above all his faults and emotional problems. It merely implies that he refuses to be paralyzed by them. He is determined to accept himself as he is but also to assume more and more control of his life.

According to Harris, there are four basic attitudes or positions which we take with regard to ourselves and others:

(1) I'm not O.K.—You're O.K.
(2) I'm not O.K.—You're not O.K.
(3) I'm O.K.—You're not O.K.
(4) I'm O.K.—You're O.K.

The first position is the universal position of every child at age five. He has been almost totally dependent on others and so his deepest feelings at this time in his life are usually feelings of dependence and inadequacy, and a strong need for approval from those upon whom he depends. Harris says that, although the words stick in his throat, there is no such thing as a happy childhood. The messages which have been recorded in us during these first five years all emphasize our dependency, inadequacy and deficiency. Some parental messages are affirming, but most of them are not. And so the first conclusion we come to about ourselves is: I'm not O.K. I can't do anything right. And the first question we ask is: What can I possibly do to please you?

The extent to which we have remained stuck in this first position of non-okayness is indicated by definite symptoms: We feel inferior in dealing with others. We need the approval of others very badly. We have problems with jealousy. We have an insatiable ambition to be as O.K. as others, as wealthy, intelligent or good-looking as others are. This ambition is usually directed to those who are close and important to us. To the extent that we have not moved out of this first position, we tend to live in a fantasy world, to experience hostility, depression and even despair.

If a child is not given sufficient recognition and love ("stroking"), position one becomes position two very early in life. The second position is basically one of withdrawal because positive strokes of praise and affection have been withheld. The inner attitude is: "I'm not O.K., but you're not O.K. either because you have hurt me. You have not loved me." And if a child is severely mistreated ("brutal stroking"), it is likely that he will move into the third position, a vindictive attitude: "I'm O.K. and you're not O.K., and it's going to cost you." In the attitude of Papillon: "You dished out all you had, and I'm still alive."

All of these first three positions are unconsciously adopted. They are based on feelings which are largely subconscious. The fourth position by contrast is a conscious decision and choice, based on thought, faith and action.

The feeling of being O.K.
does not imply that the person
has risen above all his faults
and emotional problems.
It merely implies that he refuses
to be paralyzed by them.

To make this choice effectively, we must come to a realization that there are three components in our personalities. As we have all felt at times, we are not really one but three persons all wrapped up in one. Sometimes we behave as an *adult,* who is rational and mature, capable of decisions and in conscious control of his life. At other times we seem to regress to childish or even infantile reactions, demanding immediate gratification and "our own way." There is also a wholesome side of this *child* in us; he likes swings, running along a beach, picking flowers, etc. Finally there are times when we are a living replica of our *parents,* a living composite of all their messages recorded and always playing in us.

In the terminology of T.A., these are the three familiar "ego states:" Parent—Adult—Child. They are in all of us, and we vacillate from one to another, usually without awareness unless we have worked at T.A. It is this precise awareness that T.A. would teach. Both Berne and Harris insist that we can learn to recognize the ego state in a given transaction by detectable changes in our manners, gestures, appearance, and in the very words we choose, our vocal inflections, etc.

The parent. The Parent in us is a composite of all the messages recorded in us during the first five years of life. We are acting in the ego state of Parent when our behavior is determined by these messages, which are fixed, unchanging, dogmatic. They are for the most part critical, restricting, controlling and inhibiting. Some of these messages may well be supportive and affirming.

The adult. The Adult is mature, decisive, flexible. While the Parent and Child are fixed states in which there can be no modification after childhood, the Adult is where we are open to change and growth. All hope for a different and better existence resides

118

here. The Adult in us listens to, reviews and evaluates those fixed parental messages, decides what to act upon and what to act against. From ages one to five we are incapable of evaluating what is said and done to us. We record everything as "the truth." The function of Adult, with regard to the Parent, is to reevaluate those experiences. The Adult also listens to the emotional hurts and enthusiasms of the Child, and allows or disallows the Child's whims in the light of mature values and rational decisions. It is the Adult ego state that must dominate the personality, remain in the ascendancy, or, in the language of T.A., "get plugged in."

The child. The Child in us is spontaneous, lively, creative, motivated by feelings. All emotional reactions from ecstasy to despair are stored here. The hurts acquired in our early relationships are also recorded here. The Child in us tends to be primitive and self-depreciating. Yet he is capable of excitement, wonder, and enthusiasm. The Child can bring to our whole personalities all the happiness that a lively child brings to a family group. So the Adult in us should allow the Child to express his joys and enthusiasms.

The genius of T.A. in practice is to learn how to recognize each of these states in ourselves. Parents are dogmatic and rigid. They use words like "should . . . shouldn't . . . always . . . never . . . once and for all . . . If I were you . . . nonsense . . . It must be done this way. . . ." The tone of voice is commanding or condescending. The facial expressions are judgmental, concerned, shocked, righteous, etc. The Child is found in such expressions as quivering lips, pouting, whining, temper tantrums, downcast eyes, sobbing, jumping up and down, giggling, squirming, shrieking. His vocabulary is punctuated by: "I want . . . I need . . . I wish . . . I won't . . . I can't . . . I guess . . . I don't care . . . I don't know . . . I feel . . . I am going to . . . Give me . . ." etc.

Once a person has become facile at getting in touch with his ego states, he has arrived at the possibility of emancipating the Adult, of putting the Adult in charge. He is then neither controlled by the narrow and fixed positions of his Parent nor by the insatiable needs of his Child. His life is governed gently but forcibly by reason, although at the same time he happily loves and recognizes that which is good in his Parent and in his Child. He welcomes the boundaries and wisdom of the Parent, the wonder, creativity, and enthusiasm of the Child.

We can become proficient at one of the methods recommended. With practice and perseverance we can learn to recognize the emotional forces which underlie our behavior. We can practice the needed self-discipline in acting against our emotions when those emotions would be crippling and destructive. With the help of God and those who love us, we can rewrite our "life-script." We can then move realistically towards self-acceptance, self-esteem, self-appreciation and self-celebration.

With practice
and perseverance
we can learn
to recognize
the emotional forces
which underlie
our
behavior.

CHAPTER FIVE

They were brother priests and brother Jesuits. They had for many years experienced a rich and rewarding friendship. The two had trudged together through the wilderness of the long seminary training. When one had a special need—for time, a listening ear, or whatever, the other had always been there.

The friendship was ended abruptly in tragedy and death. One of the two friends was hit by a car and killed in front of the residence where the two priests lived with their community.

When the other was informed that his friend lay dead on the street, he went running, cut through the cordon of onlookers and police, and knelt at the side of his old friend. He gently cradled the dead man's head on his arm, and before all those gaping people, he blurted out:

"Don't die! You can't die! I never told you that I loved you."

the daily bread
of dialogue

the diagnostic signs
of dialogue

As we have defined dialogue it centers around
the communication or sharing of emotions. The purpose of this dialogue is to enable the partners to
come to a deeper knowledge, understanding, and
fuller acceptance of each other in love. Dialogue is
always moving towards encounter, towards the mutual experience of each other's person through this

123

sharing of feelings. It is not for solving problems, exchanging ideas, making choices, giving and receiving advice, laying plans or reasoning things out. All these belong to discussion. Effective dialogue is an absolutely essential prerequisite for fruitful discussions.

The assumption of dialogue is that all feelings are very natural reactions that are the result of countless influences spaced out over the whole of one's life. They can be stimulated by another but never caused by him. They are in us, and most probably have been stored in us since early childhood. They represent no danger and have absolutely no moral implications. No one ever needs a reason, excuse or explanation for the way he feels. It's okay to feel whatever we feel. The only real danger is to ignore, deny or refuse to report our feelings. The repression or non-expression of emotions leads to a generalized distortion of the whole human personality and to a great variety of painful symptoms.

There is absolutely no place in dialogue for arguing since dialogue is essentially an exchange of feelings and there cannot be any argument over the way a person feels. There is room for argumentation in discussion, and couples must pass eventually from dialogue into discussion. We have to know how the other thinks, what he prefers, so that we can make plans and decisions together. Problems requiring discussion constantly enter our lives, and we must deal with them together. However, we must be sure that dialogue is really completed before discussion begins.

Finally, true dialogue is characterized by a sense of collaboration not competition. If there is a sense of contest, whatever is going on isn't dialogue. Dialogue is the simple exchange of feelings without any attempt to analyze, rationalize or assign responsibility for those feelings. If, therefore, one partner thinks that his opposite number should not feel the way he does, he has really missed the whole point. He is probably rejecting the whole idea of dialogue and probably rejecting his partner as well. However, if the couple is discovering a fresh beauty and new depths of goodness in each other's person, if they have a growing feeling of getting to know each other, they are succeeding in the art of dialogue.

motives for dialogue

Many years ago I read a book on public speaking. The first chapter was entitled: "Never Try To Be A Better Speaker Than You Are A Man Because Your Audience Will Know." It was reminiscent of Quintillian's definition of a good speaker: a good man who speaks well. The obvious implication is that our motives usually show through in spite of our attempts to camouflage them. We have all felt and been misunderstood at times, but over the long haul, the intuitions of others about our motivation are usually accurate if incomplete. People attempting dialogue should listen sensitively, therefore, to their motives. I suggest that there are three possibilities to be given special consideration.

Ventilation. When we ventilate a room, we air it out. We rid it of stale air or odors. Emotions, too, can accumulate inside us to the extent that we feel a need to ventilate them, to get them "off our chest." There may be occasional moments when this is necessary, but the fewer they are, the better the dialogue and relationship will be.

Ventilation is essentially egocentric. I want to feel better, so I am using you as a garbage dump for my emotional refuse. The occasional necessity for such ventilation is understandable, but nobody wants to be an habitual garbage dump or crying towel. Pouring out my emotional troubles to you so that I can feel better is self-centered. If it becomes a habit, a self-centered person develops, and such a person has little capacity for dialogue or love.

Manipulation. The second possible motive to be considered is "manipulation." Love, we have said, is essentially freeing. Love asks only: "What can I do for you? What do you need me to be?" The unexpressed question in manipulation is exactly the opposite: "What can you do for me?" Manipulation is a sleight-of-hand way of pressuring another into fulfilling my needs. Now, obviously there are going to be times when I need you to help me, to stay with me, to listen to me. I should feel free to ask you without fear of rejection.

Manipulation, however, as a motive for dialogue implies that one person reports and describes his feelings to the other so that the other will do something about them. The manipulator makes the other feel responsible for his emotions. For example, I can tell you that I am lonely. It is simply a fact that I am going through a period of loneliness, and I want you to know that because I want you to know me. Or I can tell you in such a way that I clearly imply your responsibility to fill the void of my loneliness. By subtle innuendos of voice, facial expression, etc. I make you feel the necessity to fulfill my needs. I am, by indirection and suggestion, using emotional leverage on you to get you to solve my problem.

There are no ways to uncover ventilation or manipulation as hidden motives in dialogue. We must remember, however, that if we fall into the temptation, we can protest our innocence to others and even convince ourselves, but others will know. Never try to be a better speaker than you are a man because your audience will know. When we are motivated habitually by the desire to ventilate or manipulate, we turn people into things. We value and deal with them only in terms of their value, function and usefulness to us. When partners in dialogue do this they degrade themselves and destroy their relationship. They soon drift off into monologue, and that is the way to alienation, to loneliness, to nowhere.

Communication. The only motive from which true dialogue can result is the desire for communication. We have said that communication means sharing, and that a person shares his real self when he shares his feelings. Consequently, the only valid motive for dialogue is this desire to give to another the most precious thing I can give: myself in self-disclosure, in the transparency achieved in dialogue.

Note. I'm sure you have felt at times, as I have, that others are not really interested in you. Not even those who supposedly love us and whom we supposedly love seem very interested in listening to us. I have certainly known many wives who feel this way about their husbands and many husbands who feel this way about their wives. The same thing is often reported to me by young people whose parents supposedly aren't interested in them. I really think that many or most of these cases can be explained by the fact that the "put off" party was using one of the first two motives for self-disclosure: either ventilation or manipulation. I know from my own experience that I get uncomfortable when I feel that I am being used or manipulated by another. I begin looking at the clock, looking for a way out. Human nature is essentially gregarious. The law of togetherness is written upon our hearts. However, this desire to know and to be known does not include the wish to be a garbage dump or a problem solver.

trust is
a choice

Anyone who has ever contemplated taking the risk of emotional transparency has also asked: Can I trust you? How far can I trust you? Will you understand or will you reject my feelings? Would you laugh at me or pity me? The usual procedure is to play swimmer, testing the temperature of the water, one toe at a time. Unfortunately, most of us decide to wait until we are sure and so never get into the healing waters of dialogue.

Waiting until we have an absolute guarantee of trust reminds me of a story I once heard. It seems that the mother of a young boy told his friends who had invited the boy to go swimming: "I am not going to allow Michael to go into the water until he learns to swim." Obviously, the only way to learn to swim is by getting into the water. Likewise the only way one learns to trust is to trust.

Dialogue cannot be delayed. The court can't bring in a verdict until the trial is held. And so dialogue demands an act of the will: I am going to trust you. I can't be sure. Perhaps you will disappoint me. But I am going to risk, to take a chance, to open my most sensitive feelings to you because I want to give you this, my most valuable gift…because I love you. Because I love you I am going to give you as my first gift, my trust.

Human nature is essentially gregarious.

the myth
of privacy

One of our strongest needs, which can easily become a neurotic preoccupation, is the need to feel safe. And so most of us like to have a room of our own with selected signs for the door, like: PRIVATE—DO NOT TRESPASS or DO NOT DISTURB. We want a place of safety, barricaded against the invasion of others with their probing questions and inquisitive desire to know all about us. There is no nakedness more painful than psychological nakedness. Out of this need to feel safe and protected from the searching eyes of another grows a myth that everyone needs his own private retreat where none but he can enter. It sounds good; it looks good; most people probably believe it. It is, nevertheless, a myth: something we wish were true, but which is really not true.

Rather than a place reserved exclusively for self, what we really need is to have someone (a total confidant) know us completely and some others (close friends) know us very deeply. The pockets of privacy which we create for a place to run where no one can follow are death to the kind of human intimacy so necessary to the fullness of human life.

First of all, and it has become a cliché by now, I can know only so much of myself as I have the courage to confide to you. If I can feel totally free with you in a place cleared of "do not trespass" signs, I will no doubt go with the assurance of your companionship into places inside myself I could never have known existed. I will go into places I could never have gone alone. I need your hand in mine and the assurance of your committed and unconditional love even to attempt honesty about myself.

Secondly, your love will be effective only to the extent that I confide myself to you. When you say in one of the many ways that love is expressed that you love me, I will want to believe that you really know me. To the extent that I have hidden myself from you the meaning of your love will be diminished. I will forever fear that you love only the part of me that I have let you know; and that if you knew the real me, all of me, you would not love me. Love follows upon knowledge, and so you can love me only to the extent that I let you know me.

It is true that, in all communication, kindness without honesty is sentimentality; but it is likewise true that honesty without kindness is cruelty. The genius of communication is the ability to be both totally honest and totally kind at the same time. Although it is one of the stern canons of dialogue that emotions should be reported at the time they are experienced and to the person to whom those emotions are related, kindness should still have much to say about the manner of communication.

But what about things that are not strictly emotions, but rather old "closed rooms" which have been a part of our human estate for a long time and which are the cluster-point of many emotions? Oftentimes these "secrets of the past" have a definite effect on one's self-image and behavior. Let us say, for example, that there is a secret shame, a humiliating failure from my past, or a neurotic inclination which I have never exposed to anyone. Perhaps if I told my partner in dialogue, he would think differently of me. He might even begin to suspect me or my normalcy.

Some say that you cannot be totally open and honest with those you love. It would destroy them. These people say that we need only to be *real* in the part of ourselves that we do reveal. For the reasons given earlier I do not believe this. I do believe that

131

these communications, which are not strictly and only emotions but which can have deep emotional implications, should be prudently timed.

Each person must make a fundamental judgment about the stability, the depth of understanding and acceptance in the relationship involved. The presumption is that these communications should either be made now, or, if that would seem imprudent, then the revelation should be made at some time in the future when the necessary depth of understanding and acceptance have been achieved. Permanent withholding will always be a permanent deficiency in the relationship, an obstacle to the love that could have been.

no judgments allowed

Of all the threats to successful dialogue, the one to be most carefully avoided is the intrusion of judgments, either about oneself or about one's partner in dialogue. We have said that no one can cause our emotions, but can only stimulate emotions that are already in us. The most common way that judgments enter into and ruin dialogue is through the door of believing that you have caused my emotions, or at least that there is such an obvious connection between your action and my emotion that "anyone would have reacted as I did." Both reactions are based on judgments and both judgments have to be false.

For example, we agreed to meet at a certain time and in a certain place. You arrive one half hour late. I am angry. I should tell you this as a simple fact, implying only that there is something in me that reacts angrily when I am left waiting. But think of all the possible judgmental accusations that could enter into my words, voice inflection, or facial expressions.

"You could have been on time."
"You acted inconsiderately."
"You didn't care about my feelings."
"You don't really love me."
"You're always late."
"You're very selfish."
"You did this to hurt me or to get even with me."
"This is why you have no friends."
"You don't think ahead."
"Anyone else would have left on time to get here," etc.

Notice that all these judgments obviously put me into a superior position in our dialogue. This is the kind of "presumed advantage" that has no place in true dialogue. You might have emotions of your own, like embarrassment or frustration; but, when I decide that righteousness is mine and suppose a privileged and superior position, it becomes obvious that my emotions must be handled, not yours. Judgments are death to true dialogue. Furthermore, the kind of judgments we are tempted to make usually involve a kind of indirect, destructive criticism that is fatal to self-acceptance, self-appreciation, and self-celebration. And when they have gone, love has been lost.

how to speak
in dialogue

The disposition to dialogue is very briefly this: I want you to know me. I come to dialogue in search of mutual understanding, not in pursuit of victory. I want to share my most precious possession, myself, with you. Emotional warning flags are fluttering all over the place, telling me that this is risky business, and I know this. But I want to take this risk for you because I love you and want to make this an act of love. I know that there is no gift of love without this gift of myself through self-disclosure.

I know also that I am *asking* through this self-revelation. I am asking first for your understanding and acceptance. I am also inviting you to reciprocate, to share yourself with me. You, too, will know instinctively a sense of risk. It may be that my taking this risk for you will empower you to take a risk for me. Whenever you are ready for that risk, I will be here for you. Do not feel that you must respond to me on my terms or at my time. Love is freeing, and so my love for you must always leave you free to respond in your own way and at your own time.

The essence of risk is this: I have needs. When I reveal my feelings to you, you will know this. I will have to tell you about my loneliness, my discouragement, my self-pity, my fears in facing life. The myth of my self-sufficiency will be exploded. I will have no more of the old facades of nonchalance or bravado to hide behind. The pretense of my self-sufficiency was both ego-supportive and ego-defensive. But it has kept you from knowing the real me. So I am going to sacrifice it for you because I want you to know the true me. When I have left all my other games, the protection of my sham and pretense, and when I have left myself naked before you, will you stay with me and clothe me with the gentle garments of your understanding?

It is relatively easy to see why this risk is necessary in a love relationship. Love, we said, asks the question: "What do you need me to be, to do?" If I am not willing to acknowledge my needs honestly and openly, then there is no place in my life for your love. You could never feel that you are really important to me. You would eventually leave me. You

134

would never want to be just another pair of clapping hands in my audience.

So I come to you in dialogue, wanting you to know me and willing to take this essential risk of transparency in the revelation of my needs. In doing so I must remember that what I will tell you is uniquely mine to offer you. The heart of my revelation will not be my thoughts. Everyone could know every thought I ever had and not really know me. I must share with you my deepest feelings. If anyone knows my feelings, he knows me. When I give you from the store of my thoughts, opinions and preferences, I somehow know that I am giving of my excess. When I give you my deepest feelings I am giving you my very substance. I am giving you the real meaning of me.

It should also be remembered that each person feels the emotions common to all men in his own unique way. My feelings of depression or hurt are not yours. It is also true that each person reacts physically in a different way. Some people develop strong bodily sensations under the influence of certain emotions, while others react to the same feelings by turning numb and freezing. Likewise, social reactions are different. When some people are hurt, they want only to be left alone, while others instinctively look for someone to whom they can describe their hurt.

So the speaker in dialogue must describe his feelings as uniquely his, and as graphically and vividly as possible. I remember when Adlai Stevenson II lost in his second presidential bid, he said he felt like a little boy who had painfully stubbed his toe. "It hurts too much to laugh, but I am too old to cry." Of course, having Stevenson's gift of eloquence would help, but each of us has to work with what he's got, even if everything he says doesn't become immediately memorable or quotable. I can still feel like "There's a funeral going on in my heart . . . I feel like a pebble on a beach . . . I feel like a cancelled stamp in the great post-office of life."

In order to achieve the quality of emotional description which will enable the listener to experience the same emotions, the speaker must first try to feel his emotions as deeply as he can. Most people don't spend enough time allowing their emotions to surface and sensitively listening to them. We are usually tempted to rush off into some distraction or into an intellectual analysis of the feelings. We never really and consciously have our emotions. It is obvious that I can communicate to you only what I have been willing to hear inside myself. If I do not listen carefully to fully emerged emotions, the sounds will be vague and my descriptions to you will be equally vague. And vague sounds do not lead to the profound sharing of feelings, the peak experiences of communication which transform and deepen a love-relationship.

I must, as a speaker in dialogue, be so vivid that you can feel and live my emotion. I don't want to tell you about that emotion; I want to transplant it into you. I want you to taste my bitterness, to wander around in the debris of my failure, to feel the pumping adrenalin of my spectacular success. In dialogue I am not telling you truths about me, but the unique truth of me at this moment in my life. Remember that it is my feelings that individuate me, that make me different from everyone else; and the feelings I am having right now make me different from what I have ever been or will ever become. I want to share with you this unrepeatable moment in my personal history.

Lastly, some kind of context for the emotional content of dialogue should be a part of the speaker's responsibility. The total communication might be

The genius of communication
is the ability to be both totally honest
and totally kind at the same time.

visualized as having three parts: (1) a brief description of yourself in terms of physical, subjective influences which might be affecting your emotional state. E.g., "I am very tired...I am on a strict diet...I quit smoking a week ago." (2) Then the specific events of the day which stimulated the emotions to be revealed. E.g., "I was refused the raise I asked for...I saw this movie and...I failed my chemistry exam...You told me you were too busy and couldn't help me." (3) The emotions themselves.

The first two points can be handled very briefly as their only function is to provide some kind of context and perspective for the emotions, which are the heart of dialogue.

how to listen in dialogue

God gave us two ears but only one mouth, which the Irish have interpreted as a divine indication that we should listen twice as much as we talk. Whether this be true or not, 50% of our personal success at dialogue is determined by how well we listen. Paul Tournier talks of the "dialogues of the deaf, in which no one really listens." If a person does not listen, it is either because he is not interested or because he feels threatened by what he might hear. Consequently, real dialogue and real listening belong to a world of understanding and love. Real dialogue can occur only here. Any suggestion or feeling of competition, of being in a win-lose contest is a certain sign that dialogue has not been achieved. Reuel Howe, in his book *The Miracle of Dialogue*, says that "Every man is a potential adversary, even those we love. Only through dialogue are we saved from this enmity toward one another. Dialogue is to love what blood is to the body."

And so the special virtue of the listener in dialogue is empathy. The true listener wants only to understand, to arrive at that moment when he can honestly say: "I hear you. I am sharing your feeling. I am feeling it with you." To do this he must be available, be called out of himself in his act of listening. He is not afraid of what he will hear because all he seeks is understanding, not victory. He has no ready suggestions, no facile solutions, and no pink pills of pity ready to dispense. He doesn't interrupt except when necessary for his own better understanding. He doesn't think about his response while the other is talking. And when the emotions of the speaker take a clear shape, he accepts them into himself. He does not merely tolerate them with a condescending: I will let you have that emotion.

Basically the true listener acknowledges and respects otherness in the speaker. Many people carry around inside themselves a little check-list with which to run others through the test of conformity. Such people prefer the whole world to be a carbon-copy of themselves. The classical figure of the non-listener, in our own current television programs, is Archie Bunker. Archie talks at people, not to them or with them. He has certain prepared answers on all topics and for all questions. He is a living portrait of the closed mind. He either knows it, or it is not important. Such a person does not have to listen.

We laugh at Archie. He reminds us of somebody we know. But, if we are starkly honest with ourselves, we will be able to admit that there is inside each of us a little Archie Bunker who really doesn't listen. He is safe and satisfied where he is. Other people are his pawns, to be manipulated into a position where they can best serve him.

Listening in dialogue is listening more to meanings than to words. It is listening with the heart more than with the head. Dialogue itself is more of a heart-trip than a head-trip. Such listening is a pondering rather than a quibbling over the meaning of words. In true listening we reach behind the words, see through them, to find the person who is being revealed. Listening is a searching to find the treasure of the true person, as revealed verbally and non-verbally. There is the semantic problem of course. The same words bear a different connotation for you than they do for me. Consequently, I can never tell you *what you said,* but only *what I heard.* I will have to rephrase what you have said, and check it out with you to make sure that what left your mind and heart arrived in my mind and heart intact and without distortion.

Gabriel Marcel says that "presence and availability" are the essence of love. I must be free (available) to leave my own self and selfish concerns to go out to you in a total readiness to listen and to be concerned (presence). While I am listening to you, you become the center of my world, the focus of my attention. My availability supposes that I am not so filled with my own emotions that I cannot leave them and listen with deep empathy to you and to your feelings. Wrenching free from the narcissism of self-preoccupation, especially when my emotions are painful, is difficult but this is a vital necessity for true listening and true dialogue. I cannot merely appear to be interested in you and what you are saying while I am in fact distracted by many other things. I must experience and convey the reality to you that my time, my mind and my heart are yours, and that there is no one more important to me in this whole world right now than you.

If I have been successful in listening, I will convey to the speaker a reassuring: "I hear you!" And his

140

Listening is a searching to find
the treasure of the true person,
as revealed verbally and non-verbally.

reaction will be something like: "Thank God! Someone finally knows what it is like to be me."

A good listener has an abiding respect for the inexhaustible mystery of the human person and its infinite varieties. Each experience in dialogue is a new discovery, an adventure into the previously unknown. He does not have definite, prefabricated, inspected-and-approved expectations or anticipations concerning the person of the speaker and his revelation. Having such expectations about what you can and cannot say gets one trapped in the "should-ought" box, and the one category that is not applicable to the riches of human emotions is that of should-ought.

Finally, a word of warning about "suppressive techniques." As everyone knows, communication can be either verbal or non-verbal. We can suppress intended communication in either way, and we probably will do so if we are threatened by dialogue. I can say something that is cynical or disruptive, or I can sidetrack you in subtle, non-verbal ways. I can yawn, look at my watch, tighten my jaws, narrow my eyes, raise my eyebrows, suddenly lean forward, change the volume or pitch of my voice. In any case I will be communicating through "coded signals," and you will know that something is wrong. Those psychiatrists who use the traditional couch usually sit out of eye-range of the patient so that none of their inadvertent reactions will be misinterpreted and cause the patient suddenly to clam up.

In evaluating our ability to listen in dialogue we should check up on our possible use of these suppressive techniques. However, more reliable than our own recognition, and certainly more important to the success of our attempts at dialogue, would be the reaction of our partners in dialogue. We should sincerely ask them how often, by what mannerisms or "coded signals" they feel "put off." Remember:

it's not what you say to people but what they hear that counts.

the case of the uncooperative partner

The objection most often raised and the question most often asked in this whole area of dialogue is this: "What if I try but my partner simply will not cooperate? He just will not open up his feelings." Many people claim to have this frustrating experience of unrequited self-disclosure, the causes of which are very difficult to diagnose.

There are, however, some presumptions and suggestions which a person in this position can investigate and evaluate with all the honesty of which he is capable. First of all, I presume that all human beings want to be open, to be known and to be loved. Loneliness and alienation are painful conditions, and will be endured only when and if something worse is feared. If my partner in a relationship remains closed, he either has or thinks he has something to fear. There is some reassurance that I have not been able to convey to him.

Most psychologists are of the opinion that, if one of the parties in a love-relationship really and truly opens up to the other as an act of loving self-disclosure, the other will soon reciprocate. The underlying reasoning of such reciprocity is: You have trusted me. I will trust you. Therefore, people with uncooperative partners might well ask of themselves the following questions:

1 Am I truly opening myself as an act of love? Or have I been simply ventilating my own emotions, manipulating my partner?

2 Have I truly wanted unity, to know and to be known, or have my efforts at dialogue really been a pursuit of my own happiness and satisfaction?

3 Do I invite the openness of my partner only through my own openness, or do I pressure him, poke with probing questions into areas that he has not voluntarily opened? Have I driven him into a defensive posture by my frontal attacks on his privacy?

4 Do I have a sense that we are collaborators or competitors? Do I want my partner to be open more for his sake or for my own? If he did open up, would I feel that it was a victory for my perseverance or his victory over his own inhibitions?

5 What suppressive techniques might I be using without even knowing it? In general do I look so depressed and fragile that no one would dare tell me the truth? Or do I look so domineering that no one would want to risk his individuality with me?

6 How have I received my partner's attempts at openness in the past? Have I ever used his self-revelation to "hit back" in an argument?

7 Have I exposed my own needs, deficiencies, and incompleteness in such a way that my partner knows that he does not have to fear me? Does my partner know of my need to know him, to share whatever he is and whatever is in him?

8 Am I, in general, the type who is always ready to give advice? Do I usually feel that I know what is best for people even when they do not realize it themselves?

9 How do I speak to my partner of the confidence I have received from others? Would he see in me a judgmental, harsh or condescending person? He may have seen the dried blood of others under my fingernails, and not wanted to risk his own tender flesh.

10 Am I too filled with my own emotions to be truly present and available to my partner?

negative emotions

Obviously, the thorniest question about dialogue is that of negative emotions. What do I do when I feel hostile or even homicidal towards you? It happens, of course, in the best of families. But there is a very definite risk and danger in telling you of my resentments, anger, bitterness or hostility, while there may be little or no risk in telling you of my grateful and loving feelings.

First of all, I feel sure that the growth of real love requires a commitment of total honesty between the two partners. They must agree from the outset that negative emotions will be just as welcome in dialogue as positive emotions. To see our way clear to this commitment of total honesty, we must face the fact that the only alternative to sharing in dialogue is somehow to "act out" these negative feelings, whether on self (headaches, ulcers, etc.) or on one another (in periods of silent pouting, in little games of spite, in the withholding of the signs of affection, etc.) or on innocent bystanders (in yelling at the children, in being irritable with people at work or school, etc.).

Secondly, we must be convinced that the "friction" of negative emotions is not a bad sign at all, but rather a sign of health and vitality in a relationship. The absence of tensions or frictions is always a bad sign: The relationship itself is either dead or dying. Where there is life there is always some vital tension. Gibran says that we can easily forget those we have laughed with but we can never forget those with whom we have wept. It is also true that every relationship must have crises. They are really invitations to rise above those soft plateaus where we want to linger permanently. Crises are definitely invitations to growth, and those who courageously accept these invitations will find a new and fresh dimension in their love-relationship.

More and more people today, educated by the world of advertisement that instant success and gratification are a law of life, are quitting, backing out of their love-commitments without ever really challenging themselves and their coping abilities. Almost as sad are those who refuse to have a crisis because they will not endure the painful tensions which are part of a growing love-relationship. They sadly settle for that twilight zone called "truce."

However, if you have really been buying what I have been selling, it will be clear that there is very little danger of overheating through the communication of negative emotions. I have been selling as fact that no one causes our emotions and that all other judgments, accusations and assignments of responsibility are alien to true dialogue. "So I'm angry," says the master of the dialogical art. "I'm angry because you were late. I well know that this anger is simply my reaction to the situation because of something in me. I also know that there are others, less scarred than I psychologically, who would react differently, maybe even sympathetically. But this is me at this moment in my life. I feel angry and even vindictive. I feel a vengeful urge to put you through some kind of frustration or inconvenience,

146

to make you wait on a lonely street corner for me. Of course, I won't do this. My emotions don't make my decisions for me. However, I just wanted you to know that this is how I feel. I've got anger and vengeance in me, I guess, and I want you to know that because I want you to know me."

a healing question

It is not strictly a part of dialogue, since it involves judgments and a decision, but it is an almost magical enabler and facilitator of dialogue. It is the simple request: "Will you forgive me?" The beginning of most human rifts that sabotage love and dialogue is what I have called a "wounded spirit." For example, I speak to you in a manner or I say something to you that hurts. I may or may not realize the effects of my manner or words on you, but to a greater or lesser degree you are crushed. It may also happen that you do not tell me of your pain, but act it out on me. We can then easily be trapped in a getting-even game, a back and forth contest. When this begins, the lines of communication are down, the relationship is bleeding and there is great need for healing.

What I am suggesting here is that most ailing relationships can be restored to health almost miraculously by this simple but sincere request: "Will you forgive me?" In asking the question, I am not assuming all blame. I am not deciding who was right and who was wrong. I am simply asking you to take me back into your love from which I have been separated. The acknowledged need for forgiveness is the most effective means of restoration for wounded spirits. No relationship should go on for very long without it.

the emotional reward
for perseverance

We have said that any suggestion of competition undermines a love-relationship and the practice of dialogue. The opposite and appropriate spirit is that of collaboration. It is a spirit that takes for granted that we are commited to each other in love, that we are willing to bear each other's burdens and share each other's joys. We have lost two I's to become one We. We will work at life's challenges together. We will succeed sometimes and sometimes we will fail, but we will be together. This sense of "togetherness" may well be the nicest and most sustaining awareness we will have. It is the joy of achieving together, of collaboration, of unity.

If self-appreciation and celebration are really the beginning of love and the fullness of life, we will achieve it together. You will look into my eyes and see there the great cause you have for self-celebration and I shall see my beauty, my value in your eyes. I want to be the first of the invited guests at your celebration-of-self party. And I want you to come to my party, because without you there never could have been such a party. Where there is unity like this, the butterfly of happiness cannot be far away.

Ailing relationships
can be restored to health
by this simple but sincere request:
"Will you forgive me?"

CHAPTER SIX

If I had only a short time to live, I would immediately contact all the people I had ever really loved, and I'd make sure they knew I had really loved them. Then I would play all the records that meant most to me, and I would sing all my favorite songs. And oh! I would dance. I would dance all night.

I would look at my blue skies and feel my warm sunshine. I would tell the moon and the stars how lovely and beautiful they are. I would say "goodbye" to all the little things I own, my clothes, my books and my "stuff." Then I would thank God for the great gift of life, and die in his arms.

from a College Girl's Journal

exercises
in dialogue

testimonies
in transparency

When I began teaching in the "largest private University" in the state of Illinois, I sensed something of the blurring anonymity felt by many of the students: an absence of identity and personal recognition. I wondered what I would do to contribute to a solution of this problem, and decided that the very least would be to learn the first and last names of all my students. So I brought a Polaroid camera to the first class of each course, posed my students in groups of six and had them write their names of the backs of the photos. On the night of the photographing I memorized all the names and faces.

For the few years that I did this, I didn't realize how much more was possible. There were familiar names and faces out there, a spirit of friendly rapport, but I was not getting to know the persons under those names and behind those faces.

So I tried a new technique to supplement the pictures. I asked each student to write a "personal journal," listening to and recording his deepest feelings on twenty topics which I listed and somewhat detailed. It was a required assignment, but I told the students I would not read them if they did not want me to. I wanted no part of confidence by coercion. As it turned out, almost everyone was either willing or eager to have me read his journal. Perhaps this willingness to take me into their confidence was a response to my own attempted openness. I had told them in class my own answers, my own feelings on the twenty topics. Transparency begets transparency. Openness is clearly contagious.

I am sure that the expected benefits accrued to the students. The unexpected was what happened to me. Suddenly persons emerged to go with those names and faces: troubled and tranquil, simple and complicated, mysterious and transparent, all at the same time. All that I had told my students about the transformation that results from peak experiences in communication was happening in me. I knew that I could never be the same again, that I could never think of "college kids" as kids again. So many of their lives had already borne adult burdens. Their emotions had been weatherbeaten by raw and raging angers, suicidal depressions, but most of all by crippling fears that the "cool look" never allowed them to express.

Our self-image and esteem is influenced mostly by those who are closest to us. In the openness of their journals, I had come close to the students, had shared their secrets. Consequently, I knew that I must reflect back to them, in my acceptance and love, a reason to accept themselves with peace and joy, to find a real cause for celebration.

Of course, the personal journals occasioned many friendships among the students themselves. There was a spirit of trust and confidence among them, and inevitably an exchange of notebooks. One of the graduating seniors asked me if I was aware that the students had come to know each other quickly and well, and that they got together outside of class and some had formed lasting friendships? I am very grateful for whatever I can contribute to the lives and happiness of my students. My teaching is an important part of my "laboratory of life," where the theories and practices suggested in this book have been tested and found helpful, at least to me.

exercise 1

an emotional inventory

It might be good to start this exercise in dialogue with an inventory-look at our own experience of various emotions. It is really very important to develop awareness with respect to our emotions. We can never really understand or share them until we begin to recognize them in our daily lives. Most people, when they first get into this "record and report" business of emotional awareness, do not realize the many shades and nuances of feeling of which we humans are capable.

The following is a partial (incomplete) list of emotions which the normal person feels from time to time. This exercise in recognition is designed to help us check up on our performance in recording and reporting our feelings. You are asked to do this by copying the number or writing out the name of the emotions listed below, taking ten at a time, and ten or more each day.

Use the following scale in rating your experience:

never	1
rarely	2
occasionally	3
often	4
very often	5
most of the time	6
almost constantly	7

After the name or number of each emotion, indicate with two other numbers from the scale above: a) the frequency with which you experience this emotion, and b) the frequency with which you report this experience to others. There may be a variation either way. E.g., It could be that you feel "angry" *very often* (#5), but you express anger externally only *rarely* (#2). Or it might be that the variation will fall the other way. It may be that you feel "depressed" *occasionally* (#3), but you talk about it *very often* (#5).

Important. After you have completed this emotional inventory, show it to and talk it over with your partner in dialogue. This inventory is designed to be an aid to self-revelation and a springboard into further dialogue. When marking the questionnaire, you might well wonder about the precise meaning or description of many of the emotions listed. It is not really important what the dictionary says. The only important thing is your meaning and interpretation. Consequently, in the dialogue which will follow the filling out of this questionnaire, you will have to explain your meaning to your partner in dialogue. You will have to explain what certain words mean to you. Feeling "angry" may mean something to one person and have another meaning for a second person. Consequently, explanation is essential. Such an exchange should invite each person to give a fuller description of the emotions that are felt and/or reported. Consult the suggestions, given in the previous chapter, on "how to speak" and "how to listen" in effective dialogue. Also try to discover the possible reasons why you feel this way, locating something within yourself and not blaming others. Also try to express the reasons why you do or do not report this feeling. Above all, concentrate on avoiding "shoulds and oughts." Remember that emotions do not have to be justified, explained or excused. There is no such thing as a moral or immoral emotion, no such thing as a reasonable or unreasonable feeling.

Example:

1. accepted   5   2

Interpretation of Example: I *very often* (#5) feel "accepted" but *rarely* (#2) report or express this feeling to others.

**emotional
checklist**

1. accepted
2. accepting
3. affectionate
4. afraid
5. alarmed
6. alienated
   from others
7. alienated from self
8. angry
9. anxious
10. anxious to please
    others

11. apathetic
12. appreciated
13. attractive
14. awkward
15. beaten
16. beautiful
17. bewildered
18. brave
19. calm
20. cheated

21. closed
22. comfortable
23. committed
24. compassionate
25. competent
26. concerned for
    others
27. confident

31. cop-out, like a
32. cowardly
33. creative
34. cruel
35. curious
36. cut off from others
37. defeated
38. dejected
39. dependent
40. depressed

41. deprived
42. deserving
    punishment
43. desperate
44. disappointed in
    myself
45. disappointed with
    others
46. dominated
47. domineering
48. eager to impress
    others
49. eager to
    please others
50. easily manipulated

51. easy going
52. embarrassed
53. envious
54. escape, desirous
    to
55. evasive

56. evil person, like an
57. excited
58. exhilarated
59. failure, like a
60. fatalistic

61. fearful
62. feminine
63. flirtatious
64. friendless
65. friendly
66. frigid
67. frustrated
68. generous
69. genuine
70. giddy

71. grateful
72. gratified by personal accomplishment
73. grudge-bearing
74. guilty
75. gutless
76. happy
77. hateable
78. hateful
79. homicidal
80. hopeful

81. hopeless
82. hostile
83. humorous
84. hurt
85. hurt by criticism
86. hyperactive

87. hypochondriacal (overly anxious about health)
88. hypocritical
89. ignored
90. immobilized

91. impatient
92. inadequate
93. incompetent
94. inconsistent
95. in control
96. indecisive
97. independent
98. inferior
99. inhibited
100. insanity, afraid of

101. insecure
102. insincere
103. involved
104. isolated
105. jealous
106. judgmental

never	1
rarely	2
occasionally	3
often	4
very often	5
most of the time	6
almost constantly	7

107. lonely
108. loser, like a
109. lovable
110. loved by another

111. loving of others
112. loyal
113. manipulated
114. manipulative of others
115. masculine
116. masked
117. masochistic
118. melancholy
119. misunderstood
120. needy

121. old beyond years
122. optimistic
123. out of contact with reality
124. out of control
125. overcontrolled
126. overlooked
127. oversexed
128. paranoid
129. passionate
130. peaceful

131. persecuted
132. pessimistic
133. phoney
134. pity for others
135. played-out

136. pleased with others
137. pleased with self
138. possessive
139. poutful
140. preoccupied

141. prejudiced
142. pressured
143. protective of others
144. proud of others
145. proud of self
146. quiet
147. rejected
148. religious
149. remorseful
150. repelled by others

151. repulsive
152. restrained
153. rewarded
154. sad
155. sadistic
156. secure
157. seductive
158. self-complacent
159. self-pity, deserving of
160. self-reliant

161. sexually abnormal
162. sexually aroused
163. shallow
164. shy
165. silly

166. sincere
167. sinful
168. sluggish
169. soft
170. sorry for self

171. stubborn
172. stupid
173. suicidal
174. sunshiny
175. superior to others
176. supported
177. supportive
178. suspicious of others
179. sympathetic
180. tender

181. terrified
182. threatened
183. tolerant
184. torn
185. touchy
186. triumphant
187. two-faced
188. ugly
189. unable to communicate
190. unappreciated

191. uncertain of others
192. uncertain of self
193. understanding
194. ungifted
195. unresponsive

196. unrestrained
197. up-tight
198. used by others
199. useless
200. victimized

201. vindictive
202. violent
203. weary of living
204. weepy
205. winner, like a
206. wishy-washy
207. youthful

never	1
rarely	2
occasionally	3
often	4
very often	5
most of the time	6
almost constantly	7

writing and exchanging "personal journals"

Most of us think that we are better speakers than writers, which may be true since we do more speaking than writing. However, I would like to put in a strong word of encouragement for doing at least some writing, especially in the beginning and during the critical times of a love-relationship.

First, there is less danger of suppressive techniques shutting off the free flow of communication. A human face has a thousand expressions, nine hundred of which can be construed as threatening. A blank page has only one look, which hasn't as yet frightened anyone. Secondly, when you are going deep inside yourself, trying to find the right words to match the unrepeatable emotions of the moment, there will no doubt be prolonged, reflective pauses. People are generally not good at waiting. The page will wait. It has, unlike people, nothing else to do.

Lastly, there are many times when the dialogical mood just doesn't come upon the two partners simultaneously. Soon promises and good intentions replace performance, and dialogue becomes one of those many things that you meant to keep in mind and get around to. Meanwhile your love life gets duller and duller. With the use of notebook journals, each of the dialoguing partners can pick his own opportune time and write for as long or as little as he pleases.

Begun in Spain, The Marriage Encounter is a movement which promotes dialogue and expression of feelings by married couples. It has been welcomed in the U.S. by thousands of couples who have benefited from its encouragement in these communication areas of the love-relationship. Most participants in The Marriage Encounter movement have found this practice invaluable and irreplaceable. Each of the partners writes every day for ten minutes in his journal, and then ten minutes are spent in exchanging journals and dialoguing on what has been written. Most Encounter couples testify that this habit of 10/10 guarantees a progressive depth of understanding, acceptance and love. The love and happiness that these couples exude seem to substantiate their testimony. I am sure that by and large the many couples I have known from The Marriage Encounter movement represent the happiest marriages and are the happiest people I know.

Marriage Encounter is for the married, but you don't have to be married to experience the value of dialogue. So find yourself a notebook, a pen, and begin now with your partner in dialogue to discover for yourselves what this kind of sharing can mean to a love-relationship. On the following pages you will find 40 suggested entry-topics. It is recommended that you take one each day. Read over the questions given there. Then listen to your own answers and emotional reactions. Try to verbalize these as vividly as possible in your journal.

Some of the suggested lines of reflection and listening under the heading of each entry-topic may seem to be directed more to the mind than to the recapturing of emotions. Please remember, however, that it is the emotional content in your answer that will be unique to you. It is through the communication of your emotions or feelings that you will most effectively be communicating yourself to your partner in dialogue. Finally, you may well find yourself with ambivalent emotions with regard to the same object or person. Each of us is a unique blend of such disparate, ambivalent emotions. We have love and resentment, certainty and doubt, joy and sadness, hope and despair arising in us simultaneously. In trying to verbalize your feelings in these journal entries be ready to welcome the emergence of such ambivalent feelings about one and the same topic.

entry-topics

1
messages on your parent-tapes

What are the most operative messages recorded in you during childhood which most influence your present attitudes and behavior? You need not remember any special words or formal statements made to you. Example is more eloquent than words. You will know which messages are most operative and influential from the recurring emotional patterns, drives, and inhibitions which you are currently experiencing. What did your parents (and other early influences) tell you about: a) You and your worth? b) Other People: Can they be trusted? Are they good? Do you have to be careful? c) Life: What is life for? Is it to win something? To work hard? To save and be safe? After you have recorded these messages, listen to and report your own emotional reaction. Do you feel sympathy, resentment, pity or what towards your parents and others from whom you heard these messages?

2
my child

The child in us is our recorded and stored-up response to the events of the first five years of life. Since most of these responses from ages one to five are on the feeling level, the child in us is our emotional storehouse, the part of us where all our emotions reside, from joy to despair. Others can stimulate but not cause these emotions to gush forth. Listen now to your child and try to describe as vividly as you can the predominant emotions of your child. These accumulated emotions, stored up in your first five years, will be recognized by the more consistent emotional reaction-patterns of your whole life since. E.g., Does your child feel rejected, lonely, inferior? Is he ever joyful, exuberant, creative, whimsical? Does he like to sing and dance? Is he ever free enough to do harmlessly "crazy" things? Does he feel "picked on," overlooked? Has he got a lot of anger stored up in him? Does he feel mostly secure or insecure, comfortable or uncomfortable?

3
the past

Do you live with warm memories of your past? Or do you fear the past, worrying that it will someday return with all its ghosts and skeletons to haunt you? Does the remembrance of past failures or guilt tug at the masks of confidence you are trying to wear now? Does the fact that you were rich, poor or middle-class, or does your ethnic background stir feelings in you now? How would you feel about going back to your old neighborhood, or seeing your grade or high school friends now? Do you experience any desire to show them what you have become? Do you enjoy or are you reluctant to talk over (share) your past with those who are closest to you now? Do you like to resurrect or would you rather bury your past? All things considered, when you think about your past, do you feel privileged or cheated, grateful or resentful?

4
yourself in two adjectives

If you were asked "Who are you?" and you had to respond by giving two descriptive adjectives rather than your name, which two adjectives would you pick? Which two adjectives best "capture" the real you and the dominant traits of your personality? After you pick two such adjectives that would best characterize you at this time in your life, describe in vivid detail what each adjective means to you. (You also might find it interesting to select two adjectives which you feel best describe your partner in dialogue and to have your partner choose two adjectives which would best portray you. It is stimulating, after we have looked at and listened to ourselves, to know how others see and hear us.)

5
ten statement autobiography

If anyone were to understand in depth the real you, what are the ten most essential things he would have to know about you? In these ten statements please do not include any obvious external facts which are visible to all who know you. Rather they should reveal the person under all the costumes and roles, his deepest reality as opposed to his surface appearance. For example, "I have always been afraid of the opposite sex...The turning point of my whole life was my mother's death...." While each sentence should express a clear and complete meaning in itself, it is obvious that this meaning will have to be filled out in the dialogue which takes place at the time notebooks are exchanged.

6
your obituary

We usually say all our nice things about people only after they are dead. We try never to say nice things about ourselves, at least not in an obvious way. In your own "advance obituary" try to work up the nerve to verbalize all that is good, decent and lovable in yourself. If you were to die at this point in your life, how would you summarize your life and your person? Do not use the usual "who—what —where—when" format. Try rather to describe who you really were, your greatest achievement, your most consistent virtue, the most unusual thing about yourself, your most endearing quality, your greatest ability, and the thing for which you will always be remembered. Finally, at the end of your obituary compose an epitaph to be inscribed on your tomb-stone which would best summarize everything. "Here lies a..."

7
greatest emotional need

In the development of human personality, depri-vation of needs, especially early in life, can leave a void which we try for the rest of our lives to filll. In one sense everyone could honestly say that his greatest emotional need is the love of another person. How-ever, love asks: "What do you need me to do, to be for you?" Of course our needs change from day to day, but what is the general answer you would give to someone who came to you in an act of love, ask-ing: "What do you need me to do, to be for you?"

8
three experiences of humiliation

Relate in your journal three experiences or inci-dents, one from childhood, one from adolescence, and one from your adult life in which you felt crushed, hurt, humiliated. Describe in detail the incident itself but especially your feelings at that time. (Sharing such experiences has an unbelievably "opening" effect on partners in dialogue. Sharing old hurts and needs somehow removes the veils of our sham and pretended self-sufficiency. It is an eloquent way of saying: "You don't have to be afraid of me. The little kid who stood there alone in the schoolyard crying is still inside me. I need you." Nothing is more reassuring to the hesitant, fearful partner in dialogue.)

9
identity niche

Each of us wants to be recognized as an individual, to find a sense of unique personal worth. Early in life we pick an "identity niche," usually a role that would be noticed and appreciated by our parents. If a given role has already been chosen by an older brother or sister, we usually look for a different niche. For example, if my older sister is the "brain," and my brother is the "brawn," I will have to specialize in something else. I may choose to be "the funny one" or the "religious" child. In the event that a person feels he has no quality or ability to individuate him, he may choose the course of what is called "negative identity," the role of troublemaker. He will get his recognition or "stroking" as disturber of the peace. Of course, these identities change during life, but it is important to recognize and to share our current inclination. Admirable as an "identity" may be in itself, it is always an obstacle to complete communication. For example, if my identity is that of being a "helper," I will derive my sense of personal worth and emotional support from this identity. Consequently, I will "edit" my communication so that somehow I will always stay in the role of helper to helped. I will not tell you of my needs, or ask for your help because that would be a reversal of roles, endangering my identity and threatening my sense of personal worth. What is your identity niche? As a consequence, what do you find most difficult to share?

10
being loved

If someone of unquestionable sincerity and sound judgment were to say to you, "I love you," how would you react interiorly? Are you able to accept love happily? Can you surrender to the joy of being loved without suspicion of mistaken identity or fear of later rejection? Do you feel just as free about being yourself with someone who loves you, or are you extra careful not to disillusion that person and lose his love?

11
strongest recent emotion

In the past six months or year of your life, what was your deepest and strongest emotion? If there were several, just pick any one. Record something of the occasion and circumstances of stimulation but mostly describe the feeling as vividly as you can, so that your partner in dialogue may experience it with you.

12
self-knowledge

How do you feel about knowing yourself? Do you like to take psychological tests, to have your handwriting analyzed? How would you feel if a psychiatrist offered to inject you with a "truth serum" and tape record your answers to searching questions about yourself, your true feelings, motives and desires? Do you have ambivalent emotions in this matter, partly curious and partly fearful of what you might find in yourself?

13
feelings about self

On a scale from 1 (lowest) to 10 (highest), rating human beings as you know them, where would you rate yourself? To call up your truest and most habitual feelings about yourself, it may help to close your eyes for a minute, and to see yourself coming out of a door, meeting there with a group of others and relating to them. Watch and listen to yourself. Watch your typical reaction when a favor is asked of you, when a compliment is paid to you, when you are criticized, when the group laughs at you. Do you like or dislike the person you have been watching? How did he seem to compare with the others? Do you feel sorry for him in some ways? Are there any questions you would like to ask him? Would you like him for a friend? Did he seem to be understood or misunderstood by others, liked or disliked by them? After you have isolated your feelings about yourself, record your emotional reaction to these feelings. E.g., I liked myself but feel embarrassed to acknowledge this. (or) I disliked myself and it makes me feel very discouraged.

14
costume

It has been said that every costume makes a statement. We are saying something and revealing something about ourselves by the colors and styles of the clothes we choose. What is your statement? Do you adopt the latest fashions, the "in" type clothes because you feel obliged to conform or is it a matter of pure enjoyment for you? Do you choose and wear your kind of clothes more to please yourself, someone else, or others in general? Do you tend to be more conservative or "mod"? Are clothes

Every costume makes a statement.
We are saying something about ourselves
by the colors and styles of clothes we choose.

to you more functional or decorative? Would you like others to turn and look at you because of your attractive clothes or would you feel self-conscious? In general, what feelings surface in you when you think about clothes and about what you are saying by the way you dress?

15
body

When you last stood naked before a full-length mirror, what were your reactions? Were you pleased or embarrassed at the sight of your body? Is the health or appearance of your body more important to you? Would you go on a "crash diet," which could possibly be harmful to your health, if you knew it would greatly improve your appearance? What do you feel when you think that someone is looking at your body? Which of your physical features do you like best, least? In what part or organ of your body are you most prone to sickness? What is your usual emotional reaction to photos of yourself? What are your feelings about "touching"? Do you feel good or uneasy to be touched? Are you a "touching" type person? If so, what do you think you are trying to say in your touches?

16
sexuality

Are you comfortable or uncomfortable with the fact that you are a sexual being? What were your feelings when you saw that this was the next topic-entry of your journal? Are you "troubled" by sexual feelings and fantasies, or can you accept them as a wholesome, natural and good part of your human nature? What does it mean to you emotionally to be a woman—a man? Do you feel secure in your femininity—masculinity? Or do you feel a need to "prove yourself"? Does your notion of sexuality pertain to something you *do* or to something you *are*? In your own mind and emotions are love and sexuality inseparable?

17
weakness

To what extent are you comfortable with your human condition of weakness? To what extent do you feel the urge to rationalize and justify your mistakes? Are you embarrassed or angered to be caught in some form of failure? How do you feel about the undeniable weaknesses of your past life? Are you afraid of future failures? Does reappearance of weakness surprise you? Are psychological (fears, complexes) or moral weaknesses (sins) harder for you to accept in yourself? Which specific weakness, e.g., shyness, explosions of temper, overeating, excessive drinking, etc. causes you the most emotional discomfort? Do you find it easier to forgive weakness in others or yourself?

18
one change in self

In your interaction with others, of which limitation in yourself are you most conscious? What is the greatest obstacle, as you see yourself, to self-acceptance, self-esteem and self-celebration? What limitation in yourself do you make the greatest effort to conceal from others? Do you feel that the one change which you would most like to make in yourself is the same as that which might be preferred by those closest to you? What feelings arise in you when you see in yourself the quality or limitation you would like to change? Do you have a sense of failure about not yet accomplishing this change? What feelings are an obstacle to making this change?

171

19
possessions

When you read the word "possessions," did you first think about material things or personal qualities and abilities? In terms of your emotional reactions, are your riches inside you or outside? Of all your material possessions to which do you feel most strongly attached? In case of a fire in your house, what is the one thing you would be sure to take with you? Describe your feelings about this object and try to explain why you feel so strongly about it. Do you ever feel that your material possessions are construed by you as an extension of yourself, so that what you are is somehow reinforced by what you have? How do you feel about showing people through your home or exhibiting your possessions? Do you ever feel a value-conflict between persons and things? When you are introduced to people considerably wealthier than yourself are your emotional reactions different than when you are meeting people at your own economic level or less well off than you? Which of your personal abilities do you most rely on, take greatest pleasure in, and would hate most to lose?

20
mine and/or thine

(This question pertains to the mutual attitudes of the partners in dialogue.) Are most of my feelings about our relative abilities emotions of competition or collaboration? Do I have a feeling of one-upmanship? Do I feel involved in a contest or unification of talents? Is it more important to me that I emerge as superior or that we accomplish together? Do we concede "areas of competence" to each other, but compete in other areas? After we have disagreed on some matter, what are my feelings when it turns out that I have been right? When you have been right? Do I truly rejoice in your successes or are there also emotions of envy and fear that your successes might overshadow my own? Does my "sex" and yours affect these feelings of competition or collaboration?

21
sources of greatest satisfaction

Enjoyment is certainly an essential part of the fullness of life. Each person draws his enjoyment, however, from his own special sources: from wandering through a forest, reading a book, clearing his desk, playing a sport or a musical instrument, conversing with a friend, etc. There is a special reward of peace at the end of a "perfect day," filled with these special sources of gratification. Describe your idea of a perfect day and the feelings special to such a day. Is the accomplishment of a task or job more satisfying to you than the accomplishment of a deep sharing with another person? Is your perfect day filled mostly with things, ideas, or persons?

22
fundamental attitude towards others

What are your anticipations in first meeting people? Do you expect to like everyone until contrary evidence excludes some, or do you expect to like only the very few who can survive your cautious scrutiny? Are you guided more by your heart or by your head in relating to people? Describe how you feel upon entering a room full of strangers. Are you initially enthusiastic about people, but feel hurt and disappointed when they prove to have real faults and limitations? Or are you rather skeptical at first and grow in your appreciation of others gradually? Whichever way you are, how do feel about being that way?

23
intimacy

Are you comfortable or uncomfortable at the prospect of being very close to another, knowing and being known as completely as possible? Intimacy has frightening aspects for everyone. What would you fear most about intimacy? Do you find intimacy easier with people to whom you are related (family) or non-relatives? How important are friends to you? If you had to move from your present location, how deeply would you feel the loss of their immediate presence? Are you more inclined to express your love for others by deep personal sharing and confiding or by doing things for them? Have you made a considerable emotional investment in your friends? How do you feel about your own present attitudes toward and accomplishments of human closeness? If you had to call someone in the middle of the night in an emergency, whom would you call and why?

24
responsibility

Do you feel an emotional compulsion to help others, even beyond reasonable limits? Do your emotions of responsibility fall in line with your prudent judgment of your capacities? Do you feel responsible for larger social problems such as city ghettos, increased crime, health care, mental illness? Do you feel an obligation to get involved politically? Do you ever feel guilty for failure to become more involved? Do you ever feel powerless and consequently relieved of responsibility? Do many or few people confide their problems to you? How do you interpret this? What does this say to you about you? What feelings does this stimulate in you?

25
sources of emotional support
Studies show that people with a greater sense of responsibility have a correspondingly greater need for emotional support from others, but at the same time such people find it harder to accept such support. Classify and describe yourself, your feelings and inclinations in the light of this statement.

26
needing others
Is it emotionally satisfying or humbling for you to need others, to have to seek their help? When helped, do you feel an urge to repay them, to balance the scales as soon as possible? Do you emotionally grasp the truth that letting others help you is a way of loving them? Are there special areas of need in which you find it emotionally difficult to ask for or accept help? Can you easily talk over your problems with another? Can you ask for and accept help in the form of listening?

27
privacy
Are there areas of your life around which you prefer a fence? When others question you about your whereabouts, activities, etc., do you feel as though you are being "frisked," invaded, or somehow threatened? Do you ever feel a psychological claustrophobia, closed-in by and overexposed to people? Do you have special techniques to defend your privacy, e.g., humor, changing the subject, giving vague and distracting responses? What are your motives for wanting privacy? Is it a learned habit from family background, or guilt feelings, or perhaps a fear of vulnerability as a result of being known?

28
dialogue

Do the bulk of your emotions move you towards or away from dialogue? What do you have that might be threatened by dialogue? What do you have to lose? Does dialogue for you represent a special risk? What are your feelings of need for dialogue? What emotional needs are you aware of that might be fulfilled in dialogue? To what extent might the self-discipline required for daily dialogue affect your evaluation of such a dialogue? How would you compare your attitude towards dialogue with that of your partner? Do any special emotions result from this comparison?

29
commitments

True love is a decision-commitment to the satisfaction, security and development of another. Once we have committed ourselves, the big question is: Are you going to be faithful because you *have to* or because you *want to*? How do you feel about the commitments you have already made? Is there more of a joyless "have to" or an eager "want to"? How do you feel when you come to the brink of a new, possible commitment? Are you frightened at the thought of irrevocability, of getting into something and not being able to get out of it? Do your commitments ever result in the "quicksand" feeling? When things are going poorly in a relationship, do you feel discouraged and impelled to back out, or are you rather determined and stimulated by the challenge? Do you ever feel afraid that somewhere in your life, through your commitments, you got off the right track and what has followed has all been a mistake?

Once we have committed ourselves,
the big question is:
Are you going to be faithful
because you have to or because you want to?

authority figures

Wherever we are, no matter how old we are, there are always authority figures: the teacher demanding homework, the boss checking up on our work, the policeman telling us to stop our cars, etc. There are basically two general reactions to authority figures of serious emotional import. The first is that of a person who tends to be a conformist, who wants to please those in authority. He is afraid of conflict, dislikes trouble. He prefers law and order, is careful to use zip-codes and mails his Christmas cards early. There is an emotion of satisfaction that comes to him in always doing the "right thing." The other basic reaction is that of the rebel. Any symbols of authority are signals to his adrenalin. Those in authority are always wrong: the President, the Pope, the Mayor, the School Principal, etc. All of them are bad news. Bosses are unreasonable and teachers are unfair. The Child in the conformist is predominantly docile, looking for okayness and approval. The Child in the rebel is angry, telling all his early parental influences, who reappear in every authority figure: "You're not O.K. You hurt me, and it's gonna cost you!" Of course, a thousand variations of these two people and positions are possible. Listen to and describe the pattern of your emotional reactions to authority figures.

31
hardest emotion to share

Sometimes we allow ourselves to experience emotions (we do not repress them), but we cannot admit or express these feelings to others. This inhibition possibly arises from our programing, some value-conflict or a fear that others would not understand. Perhaps our society or peer-group has quarantined certain emotions out of sight, such as feeling sorry for oneself or jealousy. Men are very often unable to admit fear or express tenderness. Women are often reluctant to report hostility or envy. Describe the one emotion you find it most difficult to admit and express, and as far as you can locate them, the reasons for this difficulty. E.g., I have great difficulty admitting fear because my father told me a real man is never afraid.

32
God

What emotions does the thought of "God" stimulate in you? In general, do you feel like a child in the lap of his father, a student in a classroom, a man in debt dealing with his creditor, a slave standing before his master? What does the thought of God do to you: affirm? reprehend? frighten? support? console? free? inhibit? If God had a face, describe the look he would most probably give you and then verbalize that look. What is God saying to you? Have you ever felt angry at God—a perfectly legitimate emotion—for not granting a favor or for taking a loved one in death? Do you ever feel estranged, separated, distant from God? What is your emotional reaction to theological God-talk? Could this reaction reflect some other deeper feelings in you? What were your feelings at the time in your life when God seemed most "real" to you?

33
parents

All people have a whole range of emotions stored up inside them towards each of their parents, from tender affection to bitter resentment. However, this is an area in which we have all received carefully supervised psychological programing. Our attitudes have been carefully shaped by our parents and others. Consequently we tend to edit our feelings towards our mothers and fathers, especially if the parent in question is deceased. Describe here your most basic emotional reactions to each of your parents. Remember that negative emotions are no indictment of your parents. It isn't what they said, but only what you heard that has resulted in your feelings. Is/was either of your parents a friend and confidant as well as a parent to you? What feelings were stimulated by the last question and your answer to it?

34
family

Try to verbalize the most fundamental message you have heard from your immediate family about yourself and your relationship with the members of your family. Is it a message of acceptance or mere toleration, affection or disaffection, desire to be closer or more distant, of admiration or disapproval? Remember again, you are verbalizing only what you have heard. For this you don't need a reason, proof or excuse. This is what you have heard and these are your consequent feelings. After verbalizing your family's reactions and message to you, try to verbalize your feelings and your message to your family in the same way.

Sometimes we allow ourselves
to experience emotions,
but we cannot admit or express these feelings
to others.

35
goals

No life is complete without a reason or motive, something or someone to love and to work for. What are your life-goals and what is your life-task as you see them right now? Have you made a deep emotional investment in these goals, or are they show-pieces, more a matter of lip-service than life-style? On your emotional scales what are the five things that are most important and most worth working for in life? Does your main occupation, the thing at which you spend most of your time and energy, reflect your priorities in life? Do you spend most of your time and energy on something you feel is important and valuable? How do you feel about this?

36
life-cycles

Life is a death-resurrection cycle. In every moment there is a *death*, a leaving what has been, and a *birth*, a stepping into what is and will be. We must leave things behind: the warmth of our mothers' wombs, privileged infant status, childhood toys, the irresponsible joys of youth, the protection of family and dependent status, jobs, locations, etc. And in the end, we gradually lose our physical strength, our teeth, hearing and vision. There is a constant emotional tension in most people between wanting to go back and reclaim what has been and an eagerness to embrace the new. Describe your feelings, sadnesses, fears, hopes, anticipations, etc. In going through these inevitable stages, do you feel mostly brave or afraid, mostly glad or sad, a lover of "the good old days" or do your emotions believe that the best is yet to come?

37
the future

Describe your predominant emotional reaction to your anticipated future. Are you eager for the future or afraid of the uncertainties? Do you dread the things that you see as inevitable? Calculate as best you can where you will be and what you will be doing in five years, in ten years. Is the prospect frightening, boring, dreadful or delightful? What do you feel about who will decide your future? Do you have a feeling of being in control of your life? Do you anticipate that you will determine your future? Or do you have fatalistic-type feelings that the "breaks" (good and bad) will largely decide your fate and your future?

38
growing old

What do you feel when someone asks how old you are? What age would you like to be? Someone has said that "the pessimist sees the difficulty in every opportunity; the optimist sees the opportunity in every difficulty." Does growing old seem like all difficulty to you, or are there feelings of opportunity that arise in you? Robert Browning wrote: "Grow old along with me!/ The best is yet to be,/The last of life, for which the first was made:..." What feelings do these lines stir in you? When you see aged people, what are your feelings for them? What feelings do they stimulate in you about the anticipation of being aged yourself?

39
suffering and pain

Most people are better at enduring one form of suffering or pain than another. What forms of suffering or pain are most difficult for you? Why? Is there any specific suffering or pain for which you have a particular dread or even phobia? From what do you suffer most frequently in your life? Intellectually we know that suffering can be very profitable, and we may even know that past sufferings have brought great blessings. Do you ever have grateful, welcoming feelings in the midst of suffering? If someone could offer you a pill that would have no other effect but the elimination of suffering for the rest of your life, would you take it? Why or why not? Would you give such a pill to those you love? Do you feel an inner urgency to eliminate all suffering in your own life, in the lives of those you love? Do you often have feelings of satisfaction when another person is struggling and you have hopes that he will emerge a better person? What suffering or pain in the past year of your life affected you most deeply?

40
death

In your imagination see yourself on your deathbed. The doctor says that it will be only a matter of hours now. How would you feel? Describe whatever fears, regrets, satisfactions, peace, panic, or hopes might come to you. If you were completely conscious and aware, what would you do with those last hours of life? In a separate exercise of imagination, try to visualize yourself in a doctor's office, getting the diagnosis of terminal illness, with months or maybe even a year or two to live. Describe your anticipated emotional reaction. It has been said that we all deny our mortality, that we pretend we are not going to die. Do you repress or look away from the thought of dying? Do you think rarely, sometimes, or often of your own dying? What were your deepest emotions when you most recently lost a loved one in death? Do you find the confrontation with death at "wakes" difficult? What bothers you most? Do you feel you have to or would like to say something to the bereaved family to help take the "sting" out of death? Would you emotionally rather have the one you love most in this world die before you or follow you in death? Does the thought of or belief in an afterlife actively influence your emotional reactions to dying?

exercise 3

topics for the daily ten/ten

As a final incentive for continued dialogue I would like to leave you with a list of topics for daily dialogue. I think of the forty topic-entries already given as the "essential material" of self-revelation. In a continued dialogue they should be reviewed every year, since emotional reactions and patterns change as we reshuffle our priorities and review our prejudices. However, life is filled with many other wonderful, humorous, and traumatic moments. The following questions are meant to capture some of them, but the list could never be completed. You will think of many more. Lastly, remember that anything which causes emotional reactions is a good topic for dialogue. As you get more and more in touch with your emotions your personal list of such topics will fill many notebooks. For now, look through these, choose those which resonate in you emotionally. Let each partner-in-dialogue reflect and write for ten minutes, and then spend ten minutes sharing and dialoguing on what you have written.

how do i feel when

... you surprise me with something nice?
... you seem to appreciate me?
... you laugh at my jokes?
... I think of how our children are turning out?
... I think that you are not recognizing my needs?
... I make a mistake and you point it out?
... you are holding me in your arms?
... our routines or different interests separate us?
... I am late and you have to wait for me?
... you are late and I have to wait for you?
... you have a strong interest which I cannot share?
... I try to convince you of something and you can't accept it?
... you seem to be rejecting my feelings?
... you praise or compliment me?
... I am confronted with or think of that which I fear most?
... I think that you are judging me?
... you become violently angry with me?
... I think of praying with you?
... you make a sacrifice for me?
... others notice our closeness?
... we appear as a partnership, not as individuals only?
... I reflect that you love me?
... you seem annoyed with me?
... I have the opportunity to be alone, enjoy some solitude?
... we have been separated for a long time?
... I reflect that we are growing in mutual knowledge?
... we are holding hands?
... we are making plans together?
... I am buying you a gift?

... when I think you are taking a superior role in our dialogues and discussions?

... when I do not seem able to reach you?

... you frown at me?

... you are being too hard on yourself?

... you smile at me?

... you reach out to touch me?

... I reach out to touch you?

... you interrupt me in conversation?

... we are in some form of competition, like cards or an athletic contest?

... you say "no" to one of my requests?

... I think I have hurt your feelings?

... you apologize to me?

... we can spend a quiet evening together?

... you help me locate my feelings?

... I hear from others that you have "bragged" about me?

... I hear from others that you have complained about me?

... some other interest seems more important to you than I do?

... you seem to be holding something back from me?

... I am holding something back from you?

... you look at other women (men) with obvious interest?

... others look at you with obvious interest?

... you cry?

... you are sick?

... I think about your death, and what life will be without you?

... we hear "our song"?

... you ask me to dance with you?

... you ask me to help you?

... I think you don't believe me?

... I have to apologize to you?

... etcetera

conclusion

Dialogue is to love what blood is to the body. When the flow of blood stops, the body dies. When dialogue stops, love dies and resentment and hate are born. But dialogue can restore a dead relationship. Indeed this is the miracle of dialogue.
> Reuel Howe
> *The Miracle of Dialogue*

There are no winners and losers in dialogue, only winners. Neither partner is ever required to give up or to give in but only to give, to give of himself. In dialogue we can never end up with less than we were but only more. To live in dialogue with another is to live twice. Joys are doubled by exchange and burdens are cut in half by sharing.

The listening and the speaking of dialogue, each with its own particular set of consequences, are each directed to the other. Dialogue is essentially other-centered. Dialogue is essentially an act of the purest love and the secret of staying in love.

Aren't you glad you use dialogue?
Don't you wish everybody did?

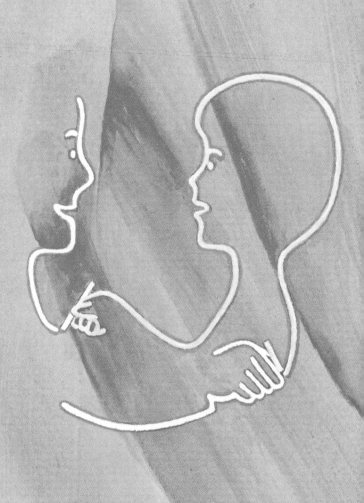

Sequel to Powell's
million copy seller,
<u>Why Am I Afraid
to Tell You Who I Am?</u>

ABOUT THE BOOK

The secret of staying in love is communication.
Indeed, our greatest gift to each other is a gift of
self through the honest sharing of feelings and
emotions. A growing relationship requires commitment
to that open and genuine expression which can
occur only in a climate of love. And, more than simply
a feeling, love is a decision-commitment, made
forever and unconditionally.

John Powell, tremendously popular with readers of
all ages, explores the fundamental prerequisite to
personal sharing: a joyful and genuine acceptance
of self, the ability to say, "I'm really glad to be me!"
The author also shows us how an awareness of our
feelings can tell us a great deal about ourselves.
This book's final chapter includes some practical
exercises which have been used successfully by
partners in dialogue to deepen their own
communication and sharing.

An irresistible blend of seriousness and humor. This
secret isn't for whispering—pass it along.

ABOUT THE AUTHOR

John Powell is an Associate Professor at Loyola
University, Chicago. Degrees in fields as diverse as
the Classics, English, Psychology and Theology
provide his powerful combination of resource and
perspective.